Praise for W.

I have known Neil for over 40 years and have followed his career as a counselor. All who have emotional wounds need to read Neil Bricco's fresh approach to old issues in *Wisdom of the Wound*. His work combines practical behavioral change with the use of "sacred space" for healing people's inner wounds.

—Dave Ditter
Retired teacher and counselor
Municipal Judge

I am a retired psychotherapist, writer, lecturer, workshop presenter, and have taught at two universities. You would think I no longer needed Neil's book. Wrong! The text, but just as much the questions at the end of the chapters have triggered me to take a closer look at some yet unhealed emotional wounds from my childhood and adulthood. Thank you Neil.

—Anna Goodwin MS, NCC
Co-author of *Sandplay Therapy: A Step-by-Step Manual for Psychotherapists of Diverse Orientations*
and author of *How to Cope with Post Trauma Stress Before it Becomes a Disorder*

I have known Neil Bricco for many years. He is one of the most enthusiastic lifelong learners I have ever known. He brings that enthusiasm to his work and takes great delight in being a facilitator in helping his clients break though old, destructive, false, worn-out ideas and beliefs into life-giving and freedom enhancing understandings of themselves and life. Neil is definitely a Conscious Creator and I recommend this book and his work wholeheartedly.

—Nancy Stetter, MA, ABS
Creative Change Life Coaching and Consulting
Facilitator of Conscious Creation Classes

I connected with Neil after my twin brother's second suicide attempt. I felt I couldn't live a good life while my brother was so unhappy. Neil has confidently led me through the maze of my own wounding, witnessing, awareness, and healing. I now embrace who I am and feel free to support others, without that haunting shame in living a good life. My emotional prison has all but vanished. I am happier and stronger than I have been in many years!

—C. Anne, current client

As a teacher in the same community where Neil provided counseling for 20 years, I experienced the benefits of his work with the children, adults, and families. Neil helped them on their healing path, and supported their personal gifts. I am grateful for your work, Neil.

—Denise Dahl-Davis M. Ed
Fulbright Scholar and Award winning teacher in Montana
Currently teaching in Istanbul, Turkey

Neil's coaching ideas helped me eliminate my biggest obstacles, which were my outdated negative beliefs about myself. He helped me get out of my own way so I could become very successful at my work as a personal trainer.

—Rick, former client

I suffered from huge swings of anxiety and depression. Neil created a safe place for me to heal, and eventually thrive. My anxiety and depression have mostly disappeared.

—Kellie, former client

Working with Neil's map to healing, I was able to release my greatest emotional pain and create positive and healthy changes in my life. I feel alive again.

—Tom, former client

Wisdom of the Wound: Discovering a Path to Wholeness

Neil Bricco, MS, LCPC

Bitterroot Mountain Publishing LLC

The author in this book does not dispense medical advice or prescribe the use of any technique as a form of treatment for physical, emotional, or medical problems without the advice of a physician, either directly or indirectly. The intent of the author is only to offer information of a general nature to help you in your quest for emotional and spiritual wellbeing. In the event you use any of the information in this book, which is your constitutional right, the author and the publisher assume no responsibility for your actions.

Copyright © 2013 by Neil Bricco

Published by Bitterroot Mountain Publishing LLC
9030 N. Hess St Ste. 331
Hayden, Idaho 83835

Visit our Website at www.bitterrootmountainllc.com

Photo and Cover by Deb Schmit
Back Cover Photo by Kathy Allen Kinman
Interior design by David E. Hibberd

Library of Congress Catalog Card Number: 2013937575

ISBN: 978-1-940025-01-8

Printed in the United States of America

First Edition

This book is dedicated to my parents Bill and Joanne,
who serve with humility,
to my siblings Andy, Robin, Cheri and Paul,
who love family and give freely,
and to all my thriving nieces and nephews.
I love you.

Contents

An introduction to the human shadow and identifying the benefits of retrieving buried shadow parts.

The Guest House

This being human is a guest house.
Every morning a new arrival.

A joy, a depression, a meanness.
Some momentary awareness comes
As an unexpected visitor.

Welcome and entertain them all!
Even if they are a crowd of sorrows,
who violently sweep your house
empty of its furniture,
still treat each guest honorably.
He may be clearing you out
for some new delight.

The dark thought, the shame, the malice,
meet them at the door laughing,
and invite them in.
Be grateful for whoever comes,
because each has been sent
as a guide from beyond.

by Rumi

"If we were talking to you on your first day here we would say, Welcome to planet Earth...your work here, your lifetime career is...to seek joy."

—Esther Hicks (Abraham-Hicks, Law of Allowing)

Introduction

It has been twenty-five years now since I started working in the field of healing and counseling. I am a life coach and psychotherapist, have facilitated small group counseling, and conducted many classes and workshops on healing emotional wounding and eliminating the blocks to wholeness and thriving. The topics covered in this book are common behavior patterns and blocks to wholeness that I have seen repeated hundreds of times over the years.

If you are a person who has been wounded emotionally by something in your childhood, past, or even in the present, this book will show you a path you can take to heal your wounds and regain wholeness.

So what exactly do I mean by the words the "Wisdom of the Wound?" To illustrate the concepts of this book I asked one of my previous clients whether I could include his story. He said, "Yes. If it can help someone, please tell it." Of course, as with all the clients mentioned in this book, I have changed his name and some of the details to protect his anonymity.

Ben came to see me one September with severe anxiety and panic attacks. Over the following months of psychotherapy he opened up and shared his history of childhood abuse. During this time he discovered many buried wounds and negative beliefs he had developed over the years. He got in touch with his fear, his rage, and his grief.

Ben and his brother grew up in a rural community and were raised by a loving but passive mother and a physically and emotionally abusive father. Ben's father, a white water river guide, worked hard all season guiding his clients through some of the most intense and dangerous waters in the west. He thrived on the excitement. But when the summer ended and fall came to the west, his father returned to a mundane life at home.

Probably feeling insecure about not working and craving the intense excitement of the summer, his father took out his fear and rage on Ben and his mother. He ridiculed and belittled them and without warning he lashed out and beat Ben severely. Ben never knew why. Years later he discovered that his father had a bi-polar disorder. Knowing his father's history helped Ben deal with his abuse.

Ben grew up afraid and doubting himself, dreading every autumn. To survive and thrive Ben buried all his childhood pain and resentment and became a competent overachiever and athlete well liked by his peers. He developed his skills as a white water guide early in adulthood, not aware at the time that he desperately needed his father's approval and unconsciously thought his choice of jobs would convince his dad that he was a "good" person. But it didn't work.

Later, Ben became a successful businessman but his emotional wounds and negative beliefs about himself continued to resurface. Over the next several years, no longer capable of suppressing his emotions, Ben's fits of rage with swings of anxiety and panic attacks destroyed his relationships and took over his life.

During months of psychotherapy he explored and witnessed his wounding, released his emotions and grieved the loss of the childhood he so desperately had wanted. Through the process he discovered that as a child he had created many negative beliefs about himself and about life. What he had learned was that regardless of how hard he tried he was never good enough to earn his father's love. Because of his guilt and shame at not being perfect he placed tremendous and unrealistic expectations on himself.

When he turned inward he retrieved the lost and buried parts of his personality, even the ones he did not like. He regained his own voice, personal power, and trust in himself. By healing his own emotional wounds with self-love and acceptance, he became a compassionate loving person again.

One fall day I received a phone call from Ben. "Something very new and exciting happened today, Neil," he said. "I was walking down the street and I realized I was smiling and appreciating this beautiful fall day. For the first time in my life I'm loving this season!"

By taking the courageous path inward through his own wounds Ben gained the "Wisdom of the Wound." He returned to living in his own wholeness and learned how to love himself. Today he looks forward to the fall and appreciates each season as it arrives.

I believe all human beings possess a soul, or psyche, and that we all enter this world in our wholeness—a full circle, so to speak. This full circle includes pure wisdom and love and potentials that help us thrive in our lives. By the time we are eighteen or twenty years old, we are perhaps half of that circle.

Throughout childhood we end up denying and burying parts of ourselves. I like the image of an eclipse or half-moon, with half of it shaded in darkness. The shaded side is not gone, just hidden from our view.

Both positive and negative experiences help create the shadow in the personality, resulting in the light and dark aspects of the psyche. The shadow resides in the unconscious, and the light half of the circle represents the conscious ego. After losing half of the circle in childhood, we seem to spend the rest of our lives trying to get it back. By integrating the light and the dark sides of our psyches, we return to our original wholeness, or full circle.

I also believe we are here to thrive and create and to witness others creating and thriving. This book is for people who are seeking to return to their wholeness, and who are seeking to thrive and create with more meaning in their lives. If you feel unfulfilled and are stuck by blocks to your own happiness, this book may help you.

The human spirit, our ability to respond to whatever life brings us, has always had a huge impact on my life. More specifically, in my life I have witnessed many people who have chosen to heal emotionally and grow spiritually, even from traumatic experiences.

Finding meaning is, I believe, one of the most important aspects of our lives. Sometimes this entails finding meaning in our suffering. Sometimes it's the purpose we find in our work, or in discovering the thing that stirs our passion and drives us. I like what James Hollis says about meaning and purpose. He states, "Meaning is experienced when we are pulled deeply into something, perhaps more deeply than is comfortable. Meaning is experienced when we are stretched and enlarged. This is why meaning often comes out of our visits to the savannahs of suffering even more than the palace of pleasure. Meaning always involves engagement with mystery—the mystery which arises out of depth, out of the radical other, out of vast bounds of being."

As a psychotherapist in private practice, I combine several counseling theories that fit my personality, life experiences, and personal beliefs. I will summarize two of the main counseling theories that I reference throughout this book. It is important for us to reduce complications and to simplify our approach to personal change. Finding a philosophy and theory of personal change that fits our beliefs and personality can simplify this process. This is true when choosing a therapist, as well. Here then are brief descriptions of the two approaches.

Starting in the 1950s, Albert Ellis developed Rational Emotive Behavior Therapy (REBT). REBT is a form of Cognitive Behavior Therapy (CBT), based on the notion that underlying many of our emotions and actions are thoughts and beliefs that cause us to act in particular ways. Just as negative beliefs are the root of some of our negative emotions and actions, positive beliefs can generate positive emotions. CBT helps people learn about the beliefs that they carry about themselves, and how these beliefs affect their actions. This is what is *in* our control or, as Ellis stated, "It's not the event but our response to the event."

The second counseling theory I utilize belongs to one of my heroes, Carl Gustav Jung. Jung was a psychiatrist from Switzerland and a pioneer in the field of depth psychology, healing, and change. He did groundbreaking work in the areas of the unconscious, archetypes, symbolism, ritual, and healing. He stated, "Meaninglessness inhibits fullness of life and therefore is equivalent to illness. Meaning makes a great many things endurable—perhaps everything."

Working with Jung's concepts of the unconscious can help people heal from early emotional wounding, by helping to change unhealthy motivations and negative habits that lie outside awareness. Throughout the book I combine CBT and Jungian concepts to help you explore your internal makeup, and to help you make positive changes in your life.

Perhaps the most important practice that I will talk about throughout this book is the power of choice. I encourage the practice of mindfulness, incorporating Buddhist and Taoist concepts, along with the Abraham-Hicks practice of the Law of Attraction/Law of Allowing. Mindfulness practice helps us create lifestyle choices with conscious intention, allowing alignment to our most important desires and goals. By removing many of our own obstacles, we are left with living in the flow of life and in the power of creating the life we desire.

In the book you will find several drawings of stick figures. I developed them over the years to help clients identify their wounds, their buried beliefs, their protective behaviors, and their shadow parts. I call each diagram "A Map to Awareness."

The examples I use in this book represent struggles and patterns of behavior that I have seen repeatedly over the years. Fear and protective behaviors are generally similar, but the healing path of the soul is solely and uniquely our own. If you have experienced severe trauma in your life, or if you are experiencing severe anxiety or depression, please seek the help of a medical doctor, psychiatrist, or psychotherapist. I am grateful for the possibilities of healing and change. May you find your truest path.

"When you pass through, no one can pin you down; no one can call you back."

—Ying-An

*"That which haunts us will always find a way out.
The wound will not heal unless given witness.
The shadow that follows us is the way in."*

—Rumi

Chapter 1

The Wisdom of the Wound

One day over lunch, a colleague described a powerful experience she'd had during a yoga therapy session. She explained, "I've been storing the emotional pain of my mother's death in my body." Her grief had been held, or stored, in a part of her body, and the yoga work helped release not only her grief, but other emotional pain as well. Describing the process, she said, "The wisdom of the wound came out in my bodywork session." As I wrote down the words "wisdom of the wound," I knew they would become the title for this book.

"Wisdom of the wound" describes in a general sense why we return to the wound, no matter how long ago the wounding occurred or how big or small the wound is. I'm not talking about a physical wound, but an emotional or spiritual wound— a psychic wound. All of us have been psychically wounded in our lives—whether it is an emotional wounding during childhood, hurt suffered in an intimate relationship, or even pain encountered while simply living our lives. The "wisdom" part signals the fact that every wound has a lesson to teach us.

When emotional wounding occurs in childhood, the child attempts to cope using limited skills and experience. Without proper support for and understanding of psychic pain, a child may develop many types of reactive, avoidant, and protective behaviors. As a result, she internalizes her wounds. Out of self-preservation, she buries her pain inside and carries on as if nothing were wrong. Burying her emotions and stifling her reactions to wounding situations are protective mechanisms that help her survive. Eventually the protective behaviors and buried emotions don't serve to protect her as they once did.

People often seek counseling, coaching, and/or psychotherapy in order to deal with negative events and stress in their lives, such as broken relationships, loss of jobs, or anxiety and depression. In my practice, clients repeatedly express concerns about how they can heal emotional wounding. *Where do I find the wounds? How do I get in touch with the wounds? How do I heal the wounds? Why should I go back to the wound if it is so painful?* However, the questions usually are not that direct. Instead, they are often expressed as *I'm lost, scared, or stuck (in pain) and I don't know what to do,* or *I don't want to talk about my childhood,* or *I'd rather just move forward.*

I see three reasons to get in touch with our wounds. The first reason is to heal from any traumatic or negative experiences that caused the wounds, including the release of any emotions and painful energy created during the wounding. This also includes grieving. There are many rituals and ceremonies that can help us heal from our wounds, which I discuss in the last chapter.

Second, we revisit old wounds to retrieve the buried parts of ourselves that we gave up when we were wounded. Jung identified these parts as the shadow. These can include many different personality characteristics or energies, from our creativity, assertiveness, and sexuality to our personal power, trust, and hope. There are many more examples, too many to list here. In Chapter 6, where I discuss the "shadow," we will explore in detail what we may give up or lose when we are wounded.

The third reason to get in touch with our wounds is to become aware of the beliefs and definitions of ourselves and the world that were formed from early negative experiences. We do this to expand our definitions of who we are and to realize more of our potential as complete human beings. As a result, we may change some of our current choices and outdated behaviors that no longer serve us.

By returning to the wounds to heal and grieve, by retrieving the lost parts of ourselves, and by reviewing and revising our beliefs and actions, we gain the wisdom of the wound. As a result, we are freed to live in our wholeness, in our true power. It's a sacred and a spiritual process, and also a mystery. Throughout this book, I will discuss how we can get in touch with these buried parts of ourselves and heal the wounds that we carry.

The Wisdom of the Wound

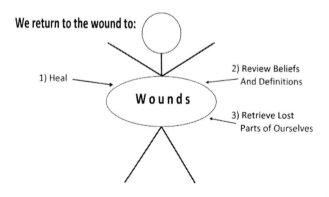

We return to the wound to:

1) Heal

2) Review Beliefs
And Definitions

W o u n d s

3) Retrieve Lost
Parts of Ourselves

Diagram 1: A Map to Awareness

We are surrounded by inspirational examples of people returning to the wound to heal and gain wisdom. Many of the most popular stories told in books, movies, and documentaries offer amazing examples of gaining this wisdom.

One such book is Viktor Frankl's *Man's Search for Meaning*, in which Dr. Frankl, a psychiatrist, describes surviving three years as a prisoner in concentration camps, including Auschwitz. Writing about his horrible experiences from personal, psychological, and spiritual perspectives, Frankl tells an incredible story of healing and achieving an understanding of human nature, even while suffering the horror of inhuman treatment. His book demonstrates that no matter how bleak our circumstances may be, we can achieve and maintain an inner state of well-being, and that even the worst suffering can be transformed into profound healing.

Dr. Frankl's book touched the lives of millions of people. He also turned his unthinkable experiences into the substance of a new form of psychological analysis he called Logo therapy. Frankl theorized that positive meaning and health can be fostered in three ways:

1. By creating a work or doing a deed
2. By experiencing a value in something or encountering someone
3. By the attitude we take toward unavoidable suffering. In his book he described this beautifully: "Those who have the 'why' to live, can bear almost any 'how'."

I believe part of the reason these foster meaning and health is that we are all continuously seeking our own meaning in life. When we can't find it, we often find illness, depression, and despair, which provide opportunity and meaning in their own way. Dr. Frankl further described the process when he stated, "The meaning of our existence is not invented by ourselves, but rather detected." Finding (or detecting) meaning, even in the suffering of the worst imaginable experiences, is required if we are to heal and thrive in our lives. Dr. Frankl's story is a tremendous example of gaining the wisdom of the wound. As he stated, "What matters…is not the meaning of life in general, but rather the specific meaning of a person's life at a given moment."

So how do we get in touch with our own wounds? Where do we find them? These are not easy questions to answer, especially in the case of childhood wounding. As I have stated, psychic wounds are elusive, at least initially. They are covered with layers of protection, such as avoidant behaviors, busyness, defensiveness, and even competence and sacrifice. The process of healing psychic wounds is very personal, different for each person. Every wound is as unique as the human being who feels it. Wounding challenges the individual's will to move forward under the weight of his past experiences, a phenomenon Jungian analyst Marion Woodman calls "psychological gravity."

The ego attempts to protect spiritual and emotional wounds at all costs, similar to how the body moves to protect a physical wound. We cover up emotional wounds and protect them with psychological mechanisms such as denial and avoidance, complicating our situation and making healing more difficult—but not impossible. Wounds can be found underneath these defensive behaviors, accompanied by sadness, fear, anxiety, anger, and even efforts to be super-responsible. We can find them behind tightness in the chest, high blood pressure, and addiction. These conditions are often symptoms of deeper wounds—painful wounds that we have run from or tried to protect since childhood.

Our culture has changed, and some traditional ways of dealing with events and emotions are no longer available. A percentage of today's psychotherapy has taken the place of past ceremonies, rituals, and rites of passage. As extended family relationships have eroded over the last hundred years or so, psychotherapy has also replaced the aunts, uncles, and grandparents who once served as wise mentors and teachers. In my practice, to help fill this gap, I try to create a "Sacred Space" in which people can be witnessed for their true and full selves. Through this process, the person learns to turn inward and witness himself in his fullness. By creating a healthier relationship with all the different parts and energies within himself, each person can learn about self-acceptance, and eventually self-love.

In Sacred Space work, I like to use the metaphor of going inward to a river inside us. The water represents all of our energies, emotions, and wisdom. When we sit on the bank and experience the river using all of our senses, we discover that our deepest energies and deepest selves find us, much like the water and energy flowing downstream toward us. By imagining the inner riverbank with conscious intention, we let these parts of ourselves find us.

But like some rivers, we may discover the water flow is sluggish. We look upriver and see a log jam. This inner logjam is holding back all the energy and water upstream. The logs represent our inner blocks, such as fears, denials and defenses, negative emotions, beliefs, pictures, and definitions that we hold just below the surface of our awareness.

As we pay attention to our inner surroundings, we discover ways to remove the "logs," the blocks that are holding all the parts back that make us whole. All the energies, both positive and negative, seek to flow freely downstream. If we can improve our relationship with the energies that are part of us, we learn to accept and integrate all parts.

Choosing to discover our wounds and get in touch with them is hard enough. The next step is to do something about them, to take ownership of them. What do we do with them once we meet them? How do we heal these wounds? Which behaviors do we need to change? I believe we heal our wounds by witnessing them and our shadow. This is utterly simple, but not easy. The book is about creating an internal map that connects us back to our true natures. I present ideas and ways of thinking about healing internal wounds and making positive changes. It's about learning to let go, to grieve, and about self-love. It's about receiving the wisdom of your wounds.

"You see, when weaving a blanket, an Indian woman leaves a flaw in the weaving of the blanket to let the soul out."

—Martha Graham

Chapter 1: Review

We return to the wounds to:

- Release negative emotions and energy, and to grieve.

- Become aware of and change negative beliefs about ourselves.
- Retrieve lost and buried parts of ourselves.

We may find symptoms of the wound in these areas:
- Overwhelming emotions stuck or built-up inside a person, such as anxiety, depression, fear, compulsions, and/or addictive behaviors.
- Defensiveness and extreme behaviors (i.e., violence, withdrawal, addiction, etc.).
- Physical illness (i.e., high blood pressure, stress/tension, or accidents).

"We would rather be ruined than changed.
We would rather die in our dread than climb
the cross of the moment and let our illusions die."

—W. H. Auden

Chapter 2

The Challenge of Change

All living things move toward healing and wholeness. A finger begins to heal the moment a sliver pierces it. As soon as the sliver enters the finger, cells, and fluid move to surround the wound, and skin grows over it to form a protective layer. Eventually the body forces the sliver up and out of the wound. Similarly, a sprained ankle or a broken leg swells with blood to protect and help heal the damaged areas. The flowers of a plant move upward and outward toward the sun. A dry, wilting plant immediately responds to water.

I believe these physical movements toward wholeness and healing are similar to the movements that take place within the wounded human soul, or psyche. And yet there is an important difference: While all living beings heal spontaneously and instinctively, the human being has the advantage (or at least the option) of drawing on consciousness to aid in this process. Although we don't always utilize it, our awareness of the healing process greatly enhances our journey toward mental or spiritual wholeness. Our challenge, then, is to consciously choose how we live our lives, including our path to healing.

Carl Jung said, "The soul seeks wholeness with or without our permission." Our souls are always moving toward wholeness, whether we realize it or not. Sometimes the path to healing is long and painful. Yet these painful events present a great opportunity to deepen our experience and understanding of ourselves. This is a significant point when considering the challenges of healing and change. Our lives can certainly get complicated in layers of pain, emotional baggage, and confusion. Maybe that's why the Buddha said, "All life is suffering." Yet the choice to meet this suffering with awareness allows us to support our soul's desire for wholeness.

We complicate things by remaining unaware, unconsciously creating confusion out of our fear and desire to protect ourselves from suffering. The ego wants to protect us, but its scope is shallow compared to the soul's bigger picture of wholeness. Because of our fear and avoidance of the pain that we secretly believe will destroy us, we allow the ego to take control, thereby getting consumed in layers of negative thoughts and emotions instead of facing the pain head-on. But facing our pain squarely is the only choice that will lead to a healing path. With practice, we learn that the huge monsters we imagine our pain to be are not as big as we feared.

When we're hurting, it's natural to want to divert our attention away from painful memories, low self-esteem, negative feelings, or beliefs that we are somehow bad or wrong. But spending some time exploring these so-called negative inner energies can help us determine whether they *are* holding us back, and to retrieve any parts of ourselves they may have damaged. For instance, if a person develops a belief that she does not deserve to be happy or that life will never work out for her, her picture of happiness might be limited to simply "breaking even" or avoiding depression, rather than achieving true happiness. Spending some time exploring her memories, feelings, and negative beliefs may help her redefine "happiness" for herself.

By becoming aware of the limiting beliefs, pictures, and definitions we hold about ourselves, we put ourselves in a better position to choose positive and healthy pictures and definitions. We can then trust our feelings as a guide to where we are in the stream of life, whether paddling upriver or flowing downstream.

It takes courage to admit fear and to remain conscious in the midst of pain. When we can face the worst pain, we may find that it doesn't have to debilitate us or cause negative behaviors. In fact, facing pain helps diminish the ego's control and support the soul's "gradient toward wholeness," as Jungian analyst Marion Woodman described it. We gain power from the parts of ourselves we're able to access through facing the "demon" and pain of our wounding.

Facing any pain with awareness requires us to call up the best parts of ourselves, i.e., our voice, courage, ability to say no, creativity, or choice to take action. We gain the "wisdom of the wound" by tearing down obstacles in our lives and in ourselves. This process requires that we remain conscious and aware of what we're thinking and doing.

At times, facing our pain is overwhelming. We can't see any way to get out from under the weight and layers of a lifetime of wounding. The good news is, you don't need to undo your whole life and "fix" it all in order to heal. And you certainly don't need to apologize for all the pain and suffering in the world. When people first approach healing, they often fear that everything has to be changed all at once. This belief creates more judgment and fear, keeping them from fully committing to the healing process. If you've ever attempted to apologize for or undo all the world's pain and suffering, you know it doesn't work. To let these unrealistic expectations go is a huge relief that lightens the load and opens up a space to choose actions that are actually *in* our control.

When we relinquish unrealistic expectations, we're left with healing and responding only to the present, making healthier choices in the moment. We can then focus on ourselves, including our fears, judgments, habits, and even the deepest, darkest places inside us—no small task. But facing ourselves honestly offers the best chance to live a healthier life filled with more meaning and purpose. It's a lifelong task focused on "allowing" versus "resisting."

So the big challenge in the journey toward healing and wholeness lies in our awareness (or lack of awareness) of our basic nature—what Jung called "individuation of the Self." As I have stated, this process includes entering dark places at times. Jung warned, "That which we do not deal with consciously shows up in our lives as fate." In other words, if we don't pay attention to our needs, to our inner voice, or to the soul's calling, we may find ourselves suffering from a failed relationship or unemployment or a physical illness. Whether or not these events are in our control, they can cause unexpected depression, fear, or a personal crisis. If we do not choose self-awareness, our unconscious likely will lead us into further pain.

In other words, if we do not address our early wounds, the soul will seek a path that leads us back to them. Although this situation is painful, it too leads to opportunities for healing and wholeness, if we let it. However, at this point we may start to complicate things and interfere with the soul's work. By attempting to avoid pain, we slip away from a conflict or confrontation, or make up a different story about it in our minds. We may enter too quickly into another relationship or add another task to our busy lives. We may lie to ourselves, or drink more alcohol, or overeat in an attempt to feel better.

These actions born from fear and avoidance may relieve the pain or discomfort in the moment, but tend to multiply the mess later, leaving us with the same unfulfilled deeper needs, and delaying the soul's work of healing. Therefore it's helpful to approach change from a very basic view. Keep it simple.

Change is most difficult when fear and judgment are the greatest: fear of failure, of not being the person we thought we were, of losing someone, or of being judged. Judgments and self-punishment keep us stuck in a cycle of frustration and failed goals. Often when we are stuck, it's because we carry an outdated or inaccurate self-image, or we're struggling to comply with someone else's expectation of us. We fear that letting go of these beliefs means giving up on ourselves, admitting defeat, or lessening our worth.

The most difficult attitudes and behaviors to change are lifelong habits created out of our core beliefs. By "core beliefs" I mean deep-seated beliefs acquired throughout our childhood and family experiences. These are the beliefs to which we have the greatest emotional attachment and which comprise our most serious sense of who we are. They can be both positive and negative. Changing core beliefs is difficult—but not impossible—because we've carried them longer than any others, and many of them reside in our unconscious.

It is time to make healthy changes by allowing all of our potentialities to thrive. As we continue on the journey, we will look at ways to uncover outdated definitions, judgments, and beliefs, and to explore new and healthier options for ourselves and thus remove the obstacles to the soul's movement toward wholeness. We will learn how to reclaim our choice to allow and accept all of our traits, rather than denying them. Our goal is to develop a better relationship with every aspect of ourselves, even the parts we do not like. It's really about self-acceptance and self-love.

Our own truth, power, wisdom, and love already reside within us. They may be covered in layers of confusion, defensiveness, and outdated roles and rules, held together by fear and a perceived need for self-protection. We need to relearn to trust our own instincts and truth. As Robert Johnson reminds us in his book, *We: Understanding the Psychology of Romantic Love*, "Zen teaches that inner growth always involves an experience of 'a red-hot coal stuck in our throat.' In our development we always come to a problem, an obstacle that goes so deep that we 'can't swallow it and can't cough it up.' This 'hot coal' in our throats alerts us that a tremendous evolutional potential is trying to manifest itself." In other words, the risks are great, and so are the rewards. By getting out of the soul's way, we can begin to take positive risks by changing some of our choices, despite our fears.

"Everything is in a process of change, nothing endures: we do not seek permanence."

—Masatoshi Naito

Chapter 2: Review

"The soul (psyche) moves toward wholeness, with or without our permission."—Carl Jung

- Internal obstacles to wholeness include self-doubt, emotional wounds, and negative thoughts and beliefs. Many of these are merely symptoms of our deeper wounds, which linger beneath our awareness.

- By avoiding psychic pain, we prevent healing and wholeness and remain stuck in negative habits.

- By healing internal wounds, we retrieve lost parts of ourselves and make healthier choices.

- Wholeness includes living in our true power and trusting our intuition and authentic self.

- Making positive change does not mean getting rid of authentic parts of ourselves, such as personality traits. Rather, it requires acceptance of these parts and improving our relationship with them.

- Making positive change does include changing the negative attitudes and beliefs about ourselves, and learning to love ourselves.

"There is nothing in a caterpillar that tells you it's going to be a butterfly."

—Buckminster Fuller

Chapter 2: Worksheet

Please write down your answers to all worksheet questions in a notebook or journal so you can review them later.

List the most significant changes you have made so far.

Which parts of the process were difficult? Which were easy?

What have you learned about yourself?

What new parts of yourself did you discover?

Are there any attempts at change at which you've been unsuccessful?

If so, what prevented your success?

Which personality traits do you not like about yourself?
What do you not like about these traits? (Personality traits can't be changed. However, you can choose to behave differently.)

List choices you have made that you felt were unsuccessful.

Why were these choices unsuccessful?

List your greatest fears in life.

When and where did these fears originate?

Have your fears influenced any of your personal beliefs? If so, how?

What would you like to change in your life (either internally or externally)?

What is preventing you from attempting these changes?

Which parts of your personality or other places inside you make you uncomfortable or scare you?

"The purpose of our lives is to be happy."

—Dalai Lama

Chapter 3

Early Wounding and the Origin of the Belief System

Throughout our lives we are shaped by both positive and negative experiences. The quality of life we lead can be determined by how we respond to our experiences, including trauma. We can't change our past, but we do have many choices in how to respond to it. Abuse and neglect are always hurtful, but a positive response can allow for personal growth from these experiences. To create meaningful change, we must focus on those choices that are within our control rather than fixating on the past. The past is out of our control. Past wounding requires acknowledgment and healing in the present because whether we admit it or not, many of our adult actions and interactions result from compensatory reactions to negative childhood experiences.

Early in life we learn about physical pain. If you put your hand on a hot stove, you pull it away. It's a natural human response to recoil from pain. We respond to emotional pain in a similar way, by trying to avoid painful emotions. Unlike avoiding physical pain, however, avoiding emotional pain can have negative consequences. When children are emotionally wounded, they tend to push the negative feelings and memories deep inside themselves so they don't have to feel the pain. This is a protective mechanism that relieves the pain in the moment, but may create a negative habit that isn't helpful in the long run.

Emotionally wounded children may begin to judge themselves as bad people. Believing you're a bad person runs a lot deeper than thinking you made a bad choice. "I *made* a mistake" is very different from "I *am* a mistake." Based on limited understanding, experience, and egocentrism, children create their own definitions of men, women, fathers, mothers, sons, daughters, success, failure, money, power, sex, and relationship. They form beliefs about who they are in relation to all these things, what they deserve, what their abilities are, or what their potential is. If we were deeply wounded as children, by adulthood we may be carrying a huge emotional stockpile of which we are entirely unaware.

We protect ourselves from childhood pain by storing the memories outside of our awareness. Our rational and conscious adult mind retains some memories of childhood, but may not remember some of the painful experiences, or how we interpreted them as children.

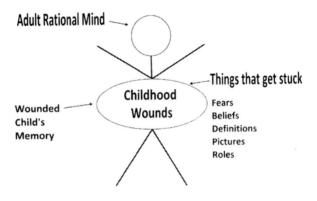

Diagram 2: Map to Awareness

Early Wounding

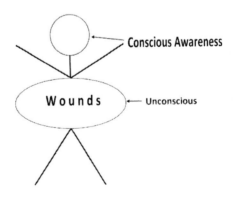

Diagram 3: Childhood

Our egos, though useful for some tasks, can keep us stuck in our own neurosis. Jung defined neurosis as "unresolved tensions between opposing attitudes of the ego and the unconscious." He also stated, "Neurosis is suffering that has not found its meaning." Without conscious and intentional healing (including grieving), the ego may attempt to avoid emotional pain. We manifest this by seeking to be liked, by attempting to look good and be accepted by others, and by taking shortcuts away from the emotional pain. In this way, the unwatched ego prevents the release of emotional pain. I believe this is what Jung meant when he said, "Neurosis is always a substitute for legitimate suffering."

We run into an almost ironic dilemma when we attempt to use the ego to examine our past painful experiences. Our ego must be strong enough to take the disruptive journey inward, yet without conscious awareness, the ego can get in the way of the healing process.

When we review our memories, wounds, definitions and beliefs in adulthood, we first run these concepts through our rational adult minds. But the rational mind is not where the wounds and negative beliefs are stuck. They are held in the wounded child residing somewhere deep inside us, often in the unconscious.

To deal effectively with a painful past, we need to return to our earlier wounding and review the definitions, beliefs, and fears that our child selves created to cope with negative experiences. These definitions and beliefs are limited and usually inaccurate because of the child's limited capacity for interpretation. The adult mind wants to cancel the child's interpretations, denying that they still have power. This is a good goal, but without some conscious work, these negative definitions, beliefs, and pictures will remain buried inside us, influencing our actions in negative and even destructive ways. I call it the wounded child dictionary.

Throughout childhood, kids experience varying forms of egocentricity. In other words, children think the world revolves around them. They take things personally, in both positive and negative ways. For instance, if a young girl's father is upset when he returns from work, the girl might blame herself for Dad's bad mood and his angry words, believing she is somehow responsible. If similar experiences are repeated enough times and the girl's thinking is left uncorrected or unnoticed, the girl might begin believing she is responsible for other negative encounters. She could construct a negative self-image from these negative (and incorrect) beliefs.

Let's take the example of Dawn, whose parents are hostile to each other and fight constantly in her presence. While angry, they belittle Dawn, taking the frustration of a miserable marriage out on her. Dawn goes to bed to the sounds of verbal and physical abuse and wakes up to cold silence or angry yelling. Her relief is to go off to school. With this little bit of information, we can guess that Dawn doesn't feel good inside. Perhaps she blames herself for her parents' unhappiness. It's likely she is burying loneliness, sadness, and resentment. It's also likely she will develop a negative self-concept from her experiences at home. She might believe that she causes pain, or that she is not a good person, and that relationships are a burden and cause pain.

Obviously, Dawn might have many other reactions, including positive ones. The point here is to see how wounding childhood experiences help form the child's belief system well into adulthood. As adults, our goal is to retrieve our power and live in our wholeness.

Early Wounding

Diagram 4: Map to Awareness: Dawn's beliefs

Childhood wounds are not buried in neat, labeled categories, but in one big pile of pain. The longer they are buried, the scarier they are when they surface, sometimes as a jumble of confused and interconnected memories. Sometimes a minor event will bump up against the big emotional button connected to our internal stockpile of pain from past trauma, resulting in a huge emotional reaction to a small or meaningless event. This trauma further encourages us to distance ourselves from the internal pain, thus staying stuck in our fear of a painful past. We may have a faint memory of not being able to protect ourselves very well as children. Thus we fear we won't be able to encounter our pain without falling apart. Sometimes, in fact, we do fall apart.

Feelings and memories can be overwhelming when they surface, especially when they have been buried for years. Picture a stovetop pressure cooker filled with boiling water. If the steam is not released, the pressure in the cooker grows to such a high level that the entire thing can explode.

It takes energy to bury pain from the past and to avoid emotional situations in the present. These efforts at avoidance may be accompanied by increased stress and feelings of heaviness. Unhealed psychic wounding results in the "psychological gravity" that Marion Woodman talks about, where we are unconsciously pulled down into depression, anxiety, or grief. If wounds and negative beliefs stay buried in the unconscious, the results can be a harmful and sometimes destructive neurosis, creating a cycle of neurosis-avoidance-neurosis. I believe neurosis supports neurosis and health supports health. If we remain in this neurosis cycle, we will attract other people who are similarly stuck in their own neurotic cycles, reinforcing symptoms of anxiety, depression, fear, and/or compulsions.

I interpret Jung's "legitimate suffering" to mean facing our painful emotions with awareness, including grief. This involves going *through* the wounds, not around them, allowing ourselves to receive their gifts. As Carl Jung said, "The road to consciousness is through the wound." When we travel this route, we gain the "wisdom of the wound."

Because the soul moves toward wholeness and healing, a person will often return to her wounds unconsciously. I've seen several extreme examples of this. The adult child of an alcoholic parent becomes an addict herself, or chooses an addict for a partner. A child who has been sexually abused becomes sexually promiscuous as an adult. A more subtle example is when a child with emotionally distant parents grows up to be emotionally distant, or chooses a partner who is emotionally inaccessible.

Protective behaviors learned in childhood become so ingrained in our habits that we scarcely notice them in adulthood. For instance, let's say you have a habit of keeping silent during conflict or when you believe people aren't respecting you. Consciously you may say to yourself, "It's just not worth the hassle to speak up" or "They never listen anyway." But unconsciously you might keep silent because you don't want to upset anyone, you're afraid bad things will happen, or you simply don't have the confidence to speak up.

Habits like this often start in childhood. There are many reasons why a habit of keeping quiet could have formed in childhood, such as having aggressive siblings, unsupportive parents, or non-communicative families. The child's unconscious memory says, "I will be punished or abandoned if I speak up." So she swallows her hurt feelings and frustrations to avoid conflict or guilt.

Over time, if the child doesn't learn to respond to her emotions in a healthier manner, she might start to medicate them with alcohol, drugs, work, sex, or other compulsive activities. Left unchecked, buried emotions may show up in the form of an anxiety attack, depression or some other physical ailment, forcing her to get in touch with the parts of herself that she has labeled "bad" or "wrong." She may also project her buried emotions (such as anger or depression) onto other people in her life.

We treat buried emotions as if they don't exist, but remember that buried emotional pain is energy. Buried emotions are in fact alive within us as energy that must be honored. For example, Tim's parents are discussing divorce, but they don't talk to Tim about it. In fact, they don't talk to him about anything. Although Tim intuitively knows something is wrong, he never hears anyone talking about the problems. As a result, because he is under stress and can't concentrate, he brings home three Fs on his report card. Both his parents blow up and scream at him, in part because of the buildup of the impending divorce. Tim doesn't know where all this anger is coming from. The next day Dad moves out. Now the parents are officially separated. Still, neither parent explains to Tim what's going on.

If nobody talks to Tim, he may conclude that his father left because he didn't get good grades or didn't behave well enough. Sound crazy? Not to a kid. I've heard many stories from adults who have carried similar beliefs around since childhood.

Early Wounding

Diagram 5: Map to Awareness: Tim's beliefs

Even children in generally positive families can suffer from poor adjustments to life. Connie grew up in this type of a family, one in which nobody ever showed anger or other "negative" emotions. She never saw her parents fight or disagree, and they always seemed calm and happy. Any disagreements between her parents occurred in private, outside of Connie's awareness.

Having witnessed neither conflict nor its resolution at home, Connie therefore never learned how to resolve conflict in a healthy way. As a young child Connie interpreted her parents' behavior to mean that they never felt upset or angry. In her limited capacity, she further assumed that it is not okay to get upset, angry, or sad. She buried any and all of her painful emotions, treating them as bad and wrong. Every time she felt a painful emotion, she thought something was wrong with her. From there, she generalized this to mean that *she* must be wrong, bad, or somehow flawed. To avoid this angst and pain, she denied having any of these feelings.

By adulthood these habits of avoidance were deeply entrenched and outside of her awareness. Connie presented an image to her friends and associates of a happy, pleasant, well-adjusted person. In private she experienced pendulum swings of depression, rage, and happiness that made her feel crazy inside. These chaotic emotional swings only served to perpetuate her belief that she is flawed. Furthermore, Connie takes these beliefs into her interpersonal relationships, finding it difficult to trust people to be honest with her about their emotions. If not addressed, Connie's negative beliefs and definitions from childhood could keep her stuck in this pattern for years.

Early Wounding

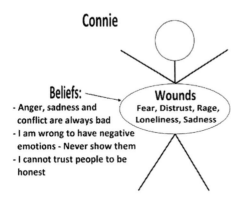

Connie

Beliefs:
- Anger, sadness and conflict are always bad
- I am wrong to have negative emotions - Never show them
- I cannot trust people to be honest

Wounds
Fear, Distrust, Rage, Loneliness, Sadness

Diagram 6: Map to Awareness: Connie's beliefs

These types of wounds can cause all kinds of avoidant behaviors. Because emotions are dynamic, they must manifest somehow. Maybe they show up in an illness, in anxiety attacks, or in a depression. A person may choose a partner who is always angry or sad, consequently projecting his or her own buried negative emotions onto the partner. All the while this person may cling to the belief that it's not okay to have negative emotions and it's certainly not okay to express them. One thing is for certain: if emotions are buried as a life habit, they will eventually show up somewhere. If we don't witness our own emotions (and buried beliefs) and take ownership in them we will unconsciously project them onto others.

It is difficult to recognize these unconscious beliefs and family roles. We've practiced them for so long, in order to protect the wounds and the ego, that they have become subtle and difficult to detect. We often cling to an unrealistic and un-healthy image of ourselves, or of our role in the family, as an inmate clings to the bars of his cell.

But hidden negative beliefs can be detected in our lan-guage, coming out in statements such as, "I can't rely on any-one" or "It'll never work out," or a private thought like, "It's just a matter of time before people find out I'm a fraud." You can hear the negative beliefs and assumptions underlying these statements.

Todd was taught to be very serious and structured while do-ing homework and household chores—even getting punished when his work wasn't performed perfectly. Wanting to please his parents, he generalized this practice to all areas of his life. His predominant personality traits included organization and structure, creating strict rules for himself and always remaining serious and disciplined.

Todd had learned to be serious and task-oriented through his school years and into adulthood as a way to gain acceptance and support from his family and teachers. By behaving respon-sibly, he avoided disapproval and abuse from his family and developed positive qualities that served him well in adulthood. However, along the way, other aspects of his personality be-came buried, such as his creative, spontaneous, and playful sides. These were equally important traits and they needed an outlet.

Predictably, Todd's serious role and strict habits did not serve him as well in all his relationships. While becoming stu-dious and reliable to suit his family, he was at the same time developing a pattern of not being able to relax and enjoy the lighter side of life. As he grew into adulthood, he couldn't un-derstand why people weren't responding to him as his parents and siblings did. People who wished to befriend and get to know him were "put off" by his rigidity and defensiveness. In spite of thinking he must always be serious and disciplined or people wouldn't like him, he actually came across as self-righteous in his belief that "most people aren't serious enough." He also clung to the illusion that he wasn't creative, friendly, or fun to be around.

Deep inside he feared being punished for exhibiting more spontaneous aspects of his personality. He couldn't relax. He became frustrated and upset when others didn't respond to him the way he expected them to or didn't appreciate his serious-ness. Todd's wounds may include sadness, fear, vulnerability, and abandonment. His negative beliefs tell him that he is not fun, creative, or likeable, and that he must always be disci-plined and perfect in his actions. These all-or-nothing beliefs are damaging and untrue.

Early Wounding

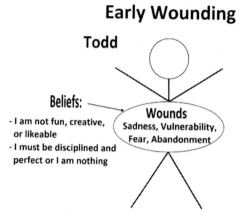

Diagram 7: Map to Awareness: Todd's beliefs

How do we let go of negative beliefs and definitions that no longer serve us? How do we let go of illusions? To begin, we want to start practicing shining the light of awareness inward toward the buried beliefs and definitions. We want to let them all come to our awareness, to invite them to the table for discussion, so to speak. It is helpful to observe our own behaviors and the effects they are having on our lives. We need to see these things clearly and honestly, which requires a close look at both our internal and external selves. For instance, for a few weeks simply observe what thoughts come to your mind throughout the day, particularly in times of stress or conflict. Are they positive or negative in nature? Are they judgmental or shame based?

Then decide if these beliefs still serve you and your deepest needs. In doing this, you'll be practicing self-awareness, a powerful tool for growth and change. It is important to remember that buried beliefs and definitions from the wounded child's dictionary are very illusive. At first you'll run them through your adult rational mind and decide that you know you are a good and competent person, or that you realize you can handle things in your life. But buried beliefs and definitions are not stuck in your rational mind, but in the fearful child's memory.

In my experience I see two symptoms of the wounded child's definitions that are universally present. One is all-or-nothing thinking, with expressions of "always" and "never", "good" and "bad", "right" or "wrong". We fear thoughts like the following may be true: "I'll never be loved." "I'll never be happy." "I'm always bad or wrong or stupid or weak...." When these judgmental and inaccurate thoughts stay in our unconscious they create a need to compensate, and our egos will attempt to protect them in unhealthy ways.

The second symptom from the inner wounded child is a sense of hopelessness. This is why we unconsciously avoid the wounding energy. None of us want to feel hopeless and pain. Because of this we often practice avoidance for years, creating more fear and making it very difficult to turn and face our wounds and negative beliefs. But ultimately the reward is our wholeness and freedom from the illusion of needing self-protection in these ways.

Feelings of hopelessness exist because the wounded child has "proof" that he will not be supported or validated because he was wounded in the past. And though we've all been wounded, the child generalizes these experiences into the all-or-nothing fear based thinking creating more compensatory and fear based protective behaviors that I address in the next chapter.

"Who looks outside, dreams; who looks inside, awakes."

—Carl Jung

Chapter 3: Review

- Carl Jung said, "The road to consciousness is through the wound." To live more consciously, to retrieve lost parts of ourselves, and to heal, we need to return to the original wounding.

- We create behaviors and beliefs that protect our psychic wounds. The protective behaviors usually involve some kind of avoidance of the painful wounds.

- In a limited way, these psychological mechanisms are natural, protective responses to wounding, like the fluid around the sliver.

- With psychic pain, we attempt to protect it with our emotions, beliefs, and actions, (through defensiveness and avoidance). But the soul will still lead us toward healing the psychic wounds, maybe not as directly as the physical wound. Because there are painful emotions and negative energies stuck in the psychic wound, the soul wants to move to release these, and to heal them.

- From early psychic wounding, we store painful memories, emotions, and negative beliefs about ourselves near the wounds.

- As adults, we may try to protect the wounds at all costs.

- Many of the negative beliefs from childhood are inaccurate or limited in scope, and are usually outside of our awareness by the time we are adults.

- Burying emotions and beliefs can create an internal "stockpile" of such things. This "stockpile" of painful memories and wounds can cause extreme reactions, such as anxiety attacks, depression, rage, and withdrawal.

- Getting in touch with unconscious negative beliefs is crucial to making healthier choices. Understanding our roles and behaviors helps this process.

- Becoming aware of undeveloped or denied parts of ourselves helps us live in wholeness.

- The wounded child dictionary holds outdated and irrational definitions and pictures of ourselves and of the world in general. These definitions and pictures reside in the unconscious outside of our awareness and adult rational minds.

- There are two symptoms of the wounded child's definitions that are universally present: all-or-nothing thinking, and hopelessness.

- By shining the light of awareness inward we release the hopelessness and binding negative beliefs freeing us from the illusion of needing self-protection.

"To attain knowledge, add things every day. To attain wisdom, remove things every day."

—Lao Tzu

Chapter 3: Worksheet

Early Wounding

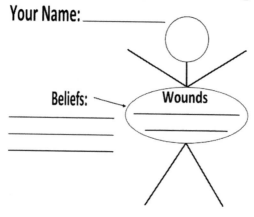

Your Name:_____

Beliefs:

Wounds

Map to Awareness: Your Beliefs

Use the above chart while answering the worksheet questions.

List any common family sayings that you heard as a child.

Did any of your beliefs come out of these messages or sayings? If so, list them.

List any childhood behaviors that you were punished for.

List any words that you were punished for saying.

What was the common punishment for your behaviors? For your words?

List any of your beliefs that resulted from these experiences.

List any childhood behaviors that you were rewarded/complimented for.

List any words you were rewarded for saying.

List any beliefs that came out of these experiences.

List any traumatic childhood wounding experiences.

What types of behaviors have helped protect these wounds?

Name any emotions that you habitually avoid. Where did you learn the rules for these emotions?

How do you typically respond to situations of conflict?

What kinds of situations do you avoid in your life?

Notice/list your thoughts, feelings, and beliefs about these times of avoidance.

What do you fear in these situations?

Consider some roles and definitions to review: husband, wife, responsible, success, money, power, sex, relationship, protection, what you deserve in life.

Is there anything you would like to expand or would you like to change any of the above definitions? If so, describe.

What kinds of childhood messages and rules did you receive about conflict? Anger? Sadness? Personal power?

List your personality traits that are positive and uplifting to yourself and others. List all of your positive personal qualities, traits, and gifts.

"The first step toward change is awareness. The second step is acceptance."

—Nathaniel Branden

Chapter 4

Old Habits Die Hard:
A Look at Protective Behaviors

Although children are resilient, they don't have the skills or the developmental capacity to protect themselves in difficult situations. Nor do they have the ability to interpret experiences and messages in an adult rational way. Children must instead learn "on the fly." Young people learn to protect their emotional wounds with many different protective and compensatory behaviors. Ultimately those compensatory behaviors must develop into mature adult responses. Thus learning about adulthood protective behaviors is very important when attempting healing and change.

As explained in the previous chapter, by "protective behaviors" I mean any behaviors or actions used to protect ourselves from emotional wounds, including negative beliefs we carry inside. The ego helps to protect these inner wounds in limited ways, both positive and negative. Protective behaviors vary greatly, from avoiding conflict and emotional pain to keeping silent, to becoming assertive, rebellious, and/or extremely competent, on a continuum from healthy to destructive.

The point here is not to label or judge our behaviors, but to better understand them. Many behaviors that were effective in childhood are less effective, even downright destructive, in adulthood, keeping a person stuck in negative habits and leading to conflict or turmoil. Discovering and understanding the unconscious motives that underlie these behaviors is extremely valuable to the process of healing and making positive change. But first we need to address the illusions connected to these habits. Let's look at some examples.

As we have seen, children learn to keep silent to protect themselves from verbal or physical abuse, to keep from getting yelled at or hit by a parent or older sibling. Silence can be very effective in these situations. But in adulthood the practice of silence no longer serves them well. The illusion that silence serves a critical need masks the fact that an adult without a voice has trouble getting his or her needs met.

Rationally the adult may know he or she can speak up without negative consequences. However, the wounded child inside remembers being punished. The inner child's fear keeps the adult stuck, torn between her desire to speak up and the habitual protective need to remain silent. Unable to draw on her personal authority and power, she will likely blame other people for not meeting her needs. By remembering and understanding the negative experiences, outdated beliefs, fears, and protective behaviors remaining from childhood, and acknowledging they are no longer appropriate, the adult can make positive changes.

Here is another example. In cases when parents are physically or emotionally absent, a child might step into the void, providing care and guidance for siblings or even attempting to rescue the parents. The care-giving child protects herself from the pain of neglect by becoming overly responsible. While being responsible is generally a good thing, it's not helpful when used to excess as a self-protection mechanism.

As the overly responsible child moves into adulthood, her unconscious identity compels her to behave hyper-responsibly at all times, usually at the exclusion of her own needs. She fears that if she fails to act responsibly, or if she can't rescue those she cares for, bad things will happen. She fears not being a "good" person. Carl Jung said, "I'd rather be whole than good," but the overly responsible child would rather be good than whole.

The fear that she is bad or has failed if she doesn't take care of others is an illusion. Nonetheless, if she makes a mistake or puts her own needs before those of others, she experiences fear or anxiety. To avoid these unpleasant feelings, she tries to keep her life in order and holds unrealistically high expectations of herself. Most likely she will not speak up, and thus will not get her own deep needs met. The adult's distant childhood memory holds a set of definitions about responsibility, power, control, and relationships. If these definitions were formed at age eight, nine, or ten, they likely are narrow in scope. As an adult the outdated definitions and beliefs influence her choices and actions. They are based in her fears of not looking good or acting responsibly to others. In order to make healthy changes she will need to redefine some of these beliefs as an adult.

The goal is not to get rid of all our protective behaviors in adulthood, but to review those that no longer serve us and replace them with healthier choices and rational, adult self-definitions. By telling our life stories, we can learn where and how our behaviors started in the first place.

In Chapter 3, I gave some examples of early wounding that may result in buried beliefs. Now let's take a look at protective behaviors that may have developed from these beliefs.

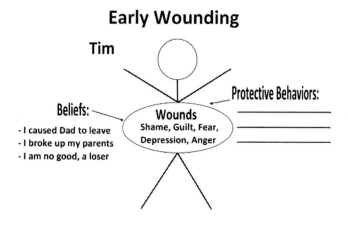

Early Wounding

Diagram 8: Map to Awareness: Tim's beliefs and wounds

In Tim's story in Chapter 3, we saw how, deep down, he felt responsible for his parents' divorce because of his poor grades and bad behaviors. To protect his wounds of shame and guilt, and to avoid causing more terrible things to happen, he strove to become an A student.

Tim's belief, "I cause terrible things to happen," is an illusion buried in his unconscious. By adulthood this illusion might spur him to be tremendously competent, highly successful, and perhaps even a workaholic, depending upon his personality, family role, and IQ. He may present an image of complete strength and competence, never showing his emotions or vulnerability, and make a habit of rescuing other people from their problems.

Most of Tim's outward qualities and behaviors are positive and healthy. Yet he also may feel tired most of the time. While he may not consciously think about his childhood fears or illusions, they nonetheless affect his adult beliefs and behaviors. As long as his wounds and negative beliefs remain buried, he is likely not to be aware that they are influencing his relationships with others.

Protecting the Wounds

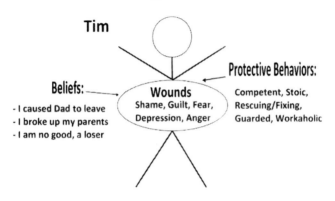

Diagram 9: Map to Awareness. Tim's protective behaviors

If Tim is content with his life, there is no need for him to change. But perhaps, for example, his wife complains that he never talks about anything personal, or that he is always away working. If Tim fears vulnerability and resists intimate relationships, these problems might be rooted in his unconscious protective behaviors.

He may feel lonely and depressed and yet continue to present an image of strength and competence. Rationally he knows he's a good, hard working person; however, buried in his unconscious is the child who believes he is a bad person.

If he chooses to return to his wounds through therapy, he could heal and get rid of some of these negative beliefs about himself. He could let go of his shame and guilt, and retrieve his voice and his true personal power. He may live with more balance, feel lighter, and discover the blessings he receives by risking vulnerability, gaining "the wisdom of the wound."

Taking positive risks might include allowing himself to feel vulnerable and communicating his fears of not being able to fix everything, or simply taking a day off or going on vacation. He might pick one of his protective behaviors (such as his rescuing or workaholic ways) and stop doing it for a while, replacing it with a more balancing behavior, such as fishing or another relaxing activity.

By changing his behaviors, Tim would likely get in touch with his old guilt and shame, which would in turn shed light on the buried judgments he carries about himself and bring him closer to healing, forgiveness, and a fuller life.

In Connie's story, we saw different wounds and beliefs. Connie never observed conflict or negative emotions being expressed in her family. Thus she learned to deny and bury her own painful emotions to avoid feeling "wrong" or "crazy."

Protecting the Wounds

Diagram 10: Map to Awareness. Connie's beliefs and wounds

Connie became an expert at avoiding conflict and negative emotions. She learned not to question people, nor to speak up, nor to express her true feelings and opinions. To support these avoidance habits, she created an image of a happy, agreeable, easygoing person. Some of her personality traits, such as her patience and ability to listen, were a natural fit for this easy-going image.

If Connie does not consciously take a look at what is going on inside, she may end up suffering outbursts of rage or anxiety attacks, or choosing a partner who is prone to these problems, thus pulling her down into her old wounds. At the same time, if she acknowledges these unhealthy and avoidant choices, she will have an opportunity to heal. By retrieving certain parts of herself (such as the ability to say no), she will gain the strength to handle conflict and tension and the chance to grieve what she lost in childhood. This is another example of gaining "the wisdom of the wound."

Protecting the Wounds

Connie

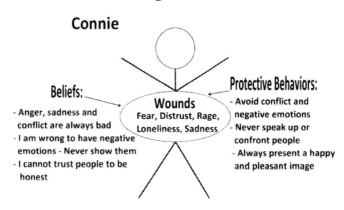

Beliefs:
- Anger, sadness and conflict are always bad
- I am wrong to have negative emotions - Never show them
- I cannot trust people to be honest

Wounds
Fear, Distrust, Rage, Loneliness, Sadness

Protective Behaviors:
- Avoid conflict and negative emotions
- Never speak up or confront people
- Always present a happy and pleasant image

Diagram 11: Map to Awareness. Connie's protective behaviors

Here is a third example of protective behaviors in action. Tom grew up in a strict patriarchal family where his father's word was the law. His father was not a great communicator and did not display his emotions, except for anger. His angry outbursts kept others at a distance. Growing up, Tom received mixed messages about anger and other emotions. Unlike his father, he was not allowed to express anger or any other negative emotions.

As a result, he suppressed anger and learned to deny his own emotional life. As a child, Tom developed a number of false beliefs. For example, he believed he caused his father's pain, and that anger and conflict are always bad. Of course, this is not true. Anger is just an emotion, neither good nor bad. Anger is only bad when it becomes abusive.

Because of these buried beliefs, Tom adopted several protective behaviors that worked in a limited fashion:

1. He learned to keep quiet, finding that if he didn't speak, he wouldn't cause conflict or make his father mad. However, this perceived control over his father's behavior was mostly an illusion.

2. To counteract his father's anger, he developed an engaging personality and a great sense of humor in an attempt to keep things "light" and stress free in the family—a strategy that mostly worked.

3. He learned to avoid conflict and anger at all costs. If anyone became upset in the household, Tom's father would trump that anger with physical abuse, screaming, and belittling. So Tom would avoid conflict to protect himself and to gain some amount of power and control. He also learned to manipulate others in order to prevent conflict. He tried to stay one step ahead of others.

Tom's behaviors served him well as a child. But as he grew older, they served him less and less. As an adult these mechanisms actually got him into trouble. Tom was not aware of the coping techniques he had developed, nor was he aware of the pain and false beliefs he had buried inside himself. The more he ran from them, the more he ran into his and other people's anger. As an adult, Tom became angry at other people for not respecting him. Actually he was disrespecting himself by denying his own truth and buried feelings.

He projected his own turmoil onto other people, and then became angry at them. In a sense, he returned to the old wounds by recreating the chaos of his youth. Because he was doing this unconsciously, nothing was ever resolved or changed.

Protecting the Wounds

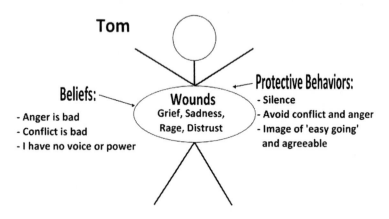

Diagram 12: Map to Awareness. Tom's protective behaviors

By choosing to return to his wounds consciously Tom would have an opportunity to regain his personal power. By grieving and releasing built-up sadness and rage, he would retrieve his authentic power and voice, learning to trust his instincts and his own inner strength. He would review his buried, fear-based beliefs about conflict and anger rooted in those early messages from his father. He would realize these beliefs are an illusion, and that his protective behaviors no longer serve him.

Because there are so many different factors influencing people's lives, it is impossible to know exactly what every individual needs in order to heal and make changes. As author Gary Zukav stated, "There are many paths to the soul." That's why it is so important for each of us to look inward and decide what approach we wish to take. We need to learn to trust our own intuition and wisdom.

Intimacy (i.e., fully connecting with another person) includes being transparent. To be transparent we need to be willing to be vulnerable. To fully connect we also must witness another person and fully see them and hear their words and meanings. I believe this is true for witnessing and validating our own inner world as well.

If we don't take time for this introspective work, we will likely grow resentful, often projecting that resentment onto those we are closest to. But when we learn to trust our instincts and speak our truth with others, we become transparent, making intimacy possible.

Many people get stuck in the habit of pleasing others at the expense of taking care of their own needs. Trying to avoid other peoples' judgments will likely take us further away from our true power. Personal power and self-respect can be lived with humility and respect for others. We need to be mindful of extreme entitlement and try to embody genuine self-respect. Ultimately this will generate respect for others at the same time.

People don't have to come from abusive families to develop negative beliefs about themselves. I hope you can see that the combination of understanding our negative beliefs and choosing different actions can help you make positive changes.

When a behavior or belief is no longer working for you, remember that it most likely served you at some earlier point in your life. You likely developed it as self-protection, or to get a need met. Ultimately our needs change throughout our lives. You may not be able to remember exactly where and why you chose these behaviors as a child. That's not required. All you need is an understanding of the connection between the behaviors you'd like to change and the beliefs that underlie the behaviors.

It may be easier at first to pinpoint the behavior than the belief behind it. The behavior is an obvious and visible action, while the belief that motivates it may be hidden. Let the behavior be a starting point for you. Look for behaviors that are getting you into trouble or that no longer serve you, particularly those involving conflict or defensiveness.

The more unhealthy choices you make, the more they support other negative choices. Fortunately the process also works in reverse: healthy choices support more healthy choices. If you get rid of one negative behavior and replace it with a positive habit, this shift will support you in making additional positive changes. For instance, if you make exercise a new habit, eventually you'll start paying attention to the kinds of food you eat. If you give up a specific negative judgment you hold about yourself, it will encourage you to let other negative choices go. It may inspire you to step further into your personal power.

Here is another unsuccessful cycle you might choose. It acts like a pendulum. If you attempt drastic and emotionally charged changes all at once, you will probably become frustrated and return to the original behavior you sought to change. This habit is based in all-or-nothing thinking. Positive changes last longer when you change one behavior at a time, rather than attempting fifty changes all at once. The greatest lasting changes occur when you let go of the negative beliefs about yourself that underlie your behaviors.

Believing that we are not worthy of happiness can greatly influence our choices. For some, this is the toughest obstacle to being conscious and observant. Practice helps. Look for behaviors that you may be using to protect yourself. Perhaps they are avoidant behaviors. Don't try to change the behavior at first. Just notice it. Notice the feelings, fears, or thoughts that accompany it. What are you trying to protect? What do you fear most in this situation?

Another approach to becoming aware is to see what types of situations or interactions cause you the most stress. Our most reactive behaviors can be a good starting point, giving us insight into our wounds and means of protection. Which behaviors, habits, interactions, or people cause the most stress in your life? Can you see any negative beliefs that may be connected to your behaviors? What beliefs do you have about your own power, about relationships, or about your emotions? About relating to other people? Which behaviors are getting you into the most trouble? How has blaming others served you? How is it currently limiting you, or holding you back? The goal isn't to find blame, but to live with conscious intention and awareness of your choices; to live a life of creating and thriving.

"We must embrace pain and burn it as fuel for our journey."

—Kenji Miyazawa

Chapter 4: Review

- "It's not the event, but our response to the event."— Albert Ellis

- "Protective behaviors" are any behaviors or actions that are used to protect the emotional wounds that we carry inside.

- The goal of protective behaviors is to protect the wounds and any accompanying buried beliefs.

- The behaviors and habits formed in childhood continue to varying degrees throughout life.

- We often react to difficult situations in "autopilot" mode; that is, in an unconscious way.

- People often resent others for not being respectful, while not respecting themselves.

- Most of our negative behaviors served us at an earlier point in our lives.

- Finding the negative belief underneath a specific behavior can help us make healthier choices, and help get our needs met.

- "I'd rather be whole than good."—Carl Jung
- The pathway to healing is through the door of vulnerability.

"I can't change the direction of the wind, but I can adjust my sails to always reach my destination."

—Jimmy Dean

Chapter 4: Worksheet

Protecting the Wounds

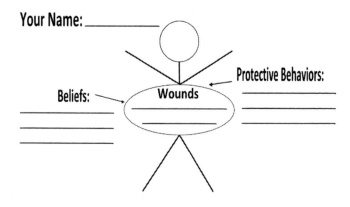

Your Name:_____

Beliefs:

Wounds

Protective Behaviors:

Map to Awareness: Your protective behaviors

Use the diagram above to help you answer the Chapter 4 worksheet questions so you can learn more about your protective behaviors. Applying the lists of your wounds and buried negative beliefs, answer the following questions:

As a child, what were your most commonly used behaviors to protect yourself and your emotional wounds in negative situations? (Examples: silence, defensiveness, stubbornness, moralist, perfectionist, workaholic, extreme helper, entitlement, righteousness, victim, martyr, fighting, joking, speaking up, competence, incompetence, defensiveness, withdrawal, etc.)

Do you still use these behaviors? Do these behaviors still serve you?

If so, which ones?

List those that no longer serve you.

List any new behaviors to replace those that no longer serve you.

List any other behaviors that you don't like.

Where did you learn them? Do they protect any wounds or beliefs you carry?

If so, what are these wounds or beliefs?

List possible illusions connected to your protective behaviors.

How do you typically act during conflict?

Where/when did you learn these behaviors? Do they protect any wounds or negative beliefs? If so, what are the wounds or beliefs?

Do you think your responses to conflict are useful?

If not, how would you like to respond during conflict?

In what ways do you think people disrespect you?

How do you typically respond to these interactions? Do you like your response?

If not, how would you like to respond differently?

What is your biggest resentment about other people?

How do you disrespect yourself in these same ways, either internally or externally?

As an adult, how do you protect your inner emotions and beliefs?

List the behaviors that don't work for you anymore.

List healthier behaviors you could choose instead.

Are these behaviors connected to a childhood negative belief? If so, list the belief(s).

List any habits you have of self-judgment or self-punishment.

Do these habits serve you? If so, how? If not, why not?

What healthy habits can you replace them with?

List all the positive ways that you would like to support yourself and stand up for yourself.

Which of these behaviors have you avoided?

What has prevented you from acting on these positive ways of supporting yourself?

"It is not your role to make others happy, it is your role to keep yourself in balance. When you pay attention to how you feel and practice self-empowering thoughts that align with who you really are, you will offer an example of thriving that will be of tremendous value to those who have the benefit of observing you."

—Esther Hicks (Abraham-Hicks, Law of Allowing)

Chapter 5

The Power of Choice

In times of conflict, adults tend to respond in habitual, unconscious ways, as they've done so many times before, perhaps since childhood. This happens for a good reason. As I've stated, at some earlier point in our lives, these protective behaviors worked. We learned them and practiced them to protect our emotional wounds, perhaps by watching a parent or older sibling.

The unconscious protective behaviors often will create anger, frustration, sadness, fear, or resentment. We may resist these painful emotions without achieving a better understanding of why they are continually resurfacing. We habitually hover around the pain, never moving away from it or through it, and never responding in a new way to conflict or stressful interactions.

Albert Einstein said, "Insanity is doing the same thing over and over again and expecting different results." These individuals who resist changes may blame their pain on other people or circumstances, rather than look at the part they play in their own situations. They don't see that they have many possible responses from which to choose.

Connie (from Chapter 3) feels disrespected by the people she's closest to. Her family and friends belittle her and do not listen to her. Sometimes these behaviors are blatant, and sometimes they include subtle insinuations of disrespect. Connie isn't sure if her friend's actions are intentional or not, but it doesn't really matter. What matters is how Connie responds. She has big emotional reactions on the inside, but out of fear and uncertainty, she keeps silent. Keeping silent is a protective behavior that is not serving Connie well. As Plato said, "Your silence gives consent." Like many people who are uncomfortable with conflict, Connie has long-running habits of avoiding conflict and disrespecting herself by not standing up for her own needs. By not taking responsibility for getting her own needs met, she consents to the negative treatment she receives. Fear and deep resentment of herself and others keeps her stuck.

Protecting the Wounds

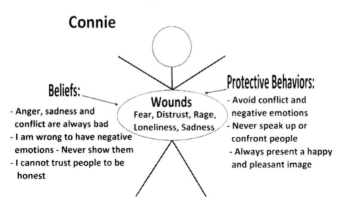

Connie

Beliefs:
- Anger, sadness and conflict are always bad
- I am wrong to have negative emotions - Never show them
- I cannot trust people to be honest

Wounds
Fear, Distrust, Rage, Loneliness, Sadness

Protective Behaviors:
- Avoid conflict and negative emotions
- Never speak up or confront people
- Always present a happy and pleasant image

Diagram 13: Map to Awareness: Connie's protective behaviors

Connie is at a crossroads. If she is able to move past her own discomfort and fear, she will see that she has a great opportunity for growth and positive change. By facing her dilemma and taking the risk of being assertive, she has a chance to heal and step into her true power. Her reward will be living in her wholeness. By retrieving some of the best parts of herself, she will uncover what she buried in childhood, including her voice, integrity, personal power, self-respect, and love of self.

She might pick one of her protective behaviors and change it. For instance, by making a decision to speak up more often, she would create an opportunity to get in touch with her fear, guilt, or shame. Why would she want to do this? Ultimately, in order to walk in her true personal power and take responsibility for getting her own needs met. To meet this goal, she will need to face her own fears and judgments. But she will also be supporting her voice, getting her needs met and regaining her personal power.

If Connie waits until she no longer feels afraid, she may never move forward. At first, there is always a certain amount of fear in turning inward. Recall that Friedrich Nietzsche said, "If you say no to any single factor in your life, you have unraveled the whole thing." I take this to mean that if Connie ignores her own fear and resentment, if she says no to her own voice and her own power, then she has "unraveled the whole thing." It takes courage to admit fear and remain conscious in the middle of pain.

Avoidance served Connie well in childhood. As an adult, the same beliefs and behaviors are usually not as effective. Connie has choices. She can choose to change her reactions by replacing an old reaction with a new behavior. She might begin by planning a response to the next instance in which she feels slighted or disrespected by others. She will no doubt still feel fear about the new behavior, but she can help herself by remembering she can be scared *without* a plan in moments of conflict, or she can be afraid *with* a plan. Obviously she has a better chance of taking good care of herself with a plan.

As helpful as a behavioral plan can be, it is even more important that Connie chooses self-respect. When she doesn't speak up, she is unconsciously acting as if she doesn't matter, which is likely an old and outdated belief. She will show self-respect by speaking up, even if she is fearful. From there she can choose friends who will support her when she advocates for herself. Connie's wounded child from long ago fears getting punished and not being able to handle the situation, but her rational and adult mind knows she can speak her own truth.

Adults who begin to make changes related to their own personal power often find the biggest resistance coming from their family of origin. Many times parents and adult siblings fight the person who is attempting to make healthy changes. The reason is simple (and painful): Family members who are stuck in old, long-running negative habits feel threatened. By choosing to live with self-respect and genuineness, a person is most likely challenging negative family traditions and behavioral habits.

It's often the people who love you the most who don't support your movement into healthier choices and ways of taking care of yourself. This is most typical when those family members don't want to face their own dysfunction. Not everyone chooses to heal or to enact positive change.

Because family members who don't want healthy change often feel threatened, emotionally wounded or abusive families frequently remain stuck in layers of dysfunction. Wounded parents may unwittingly train their children to accept chaos and neurosis as normal ways of living. Children end up not trusting their own common sense, intuition, and judgments. By the time they reach adulthood, they are stuck in old and outdated definitions of what a healthy relationship looks and sounds like. The dysfunction is treated as "normal," while the healthier actions are treated as abnormal or "wrong." This dynamic is initially confusing, as the person making the courageous step to heal is treated as sick, even while he is getting healthier.

A forty-year-old friend of mine, wanting to take better care of herself, asked her adult brother why he never called or stopped to see her when he came to town. He blew up at her and ceased all contact with her. When her mother asked her about what had happened, she explained. Her mother took her brother's side, blew up at her, and never called her again. My friend had the challenge of not feeling crazy while sorting through her anger, confusion, and grief at losing her family and giving up the neurotic lifestyle she was raised in. These are not easy challenges.

One way to learn more about negative habits is to pinpoint a common frustration you feel with a person in your life, whether it's a family member or someone outside the family. You may find your frustration lies with someone who is constantly late or who excludes you from conversations or activities, or it may be with situations in which you are often negatively treated, such as being blamed for things. Look for a common pattern in behavior. These situations may be very real, or possibly exaggerated in your own mind.

The short-term goal is to become more conscious in the moment. That consciousness includes making and enacting a plan. Ultimately the goal is to be happy and content while living in your fullness, but this new experience takes practice to realize.

Take ownership for your own happiness, for your own life. The wounded child and the ego often react, and instead of the rational adult stepping forward, you may act defensively or withdraw from life. In doing so you end up overtly feeling angry at the world and deep down resenting yourself. The sad result is the loss of your integrity and authentic power.

If you can see that you are hurting yourself and simultaneously blaming others, the cycle can be stopped. You can take full responsibility and ownership in your own power, your own life. If you can say, "My soul, my power, my value are non-negotiable" (and really believe this), you will start to change your actions. The goal is not only to say these words, but also to live and honor them. If you are not attached to every outcome that occurs throughout the day, to every competitive "win" that proves you are all right and a "good" person, you can achieve higher goals.

The ego wants to win all these battles, but the deeper desires of the soul have other plans. Think of the tremendous amount of wasted time and energy people spend throughout the days, months, and years reacting instead of acting out of choice. It's a choice to get caught up in all the mini-victories and loses and then brood about them all day. It's also a choice to heal, to see your bigger purpose, and choose a meaningful life of thriving.

"When you do things from your soul you feel a river moving in you, a joy. When action comes from another section, the feeling disappears."

—Rumi

Chapter 5: Review

Protective behavior typically evolves as follows:

- Emotionally wounded parents neglect, abuse, or are disrespectful toward   the child.

- The child buries these hurts, fears, and negative beliefs.

- Out of a need for survival/self-preservation, the child doesn't question or challenge the parents or the system. Silence and withdrawal become protective behaviors.

By adulthood, silence and withdrawal are unconscious habits of protection. The illusion is that they still work and, if they are changed, bad things will happen. These behaviors may be obvious and frustrating to other people, both family and non-family members alike.

Two common frustrations people experience in their interactions:

- Being treated with disrespect (real or imagined).
- Being excluded from events or people.

These are some emotions and reactions that may occur:
Anger, sadness, fear, blame, aggression, withdrawal.

To heal:

- Acknowledge your pain.

- Pinpoint the need(s) not getting met: e.g., respect, being heard, valued, or loved.

- Choose which action(s) will help you get your needs met: e.g., stating your needs/requests (speaking up), choosing different activities or relationships.

- Act on your choices.

Discover the buried negative beliefs you carry about yourself in relationships:

- "I don't deserve respect."

- "People will not support me."

- "I will never be loved."

How do you treat yourself in similar ways?

"Imagination is everything. It's the preview of life's coming attractions."

—Albert Einstein

Chapter 5: Worksheet

List any ongoing negative interactions you have with people.

Does this occur with several different people? Is there a common theme or topic to the conflict? If so, what is it?

What are you thinking or feeling in these situations?

List any judgments you have in these situations.

How do you most often respond in these interactions?

How do your behaviors serve your needs?

Which of your responses are protective behaviors you learned in childhood?

What happened to you as a child in your family to teach you these protective behaviors?

Are there any negative beliefs deep inside you that you carry about the situation? For instance, do you believe that you won't be respected, supported, or heard in these situations?

Do you expect negative things to happen to you? If so, why?

Do you ever treat yourself in a similar way, especially internally? For instance, do you disrespect yourself or judge yourself often?

List the ways you do this:

Are you often hard on yourself? If so, why? List examples.

What situations do you not speak up in?

How do you feel when you don't speak up? What are your thoughts?

Which of your needs are not getting met at this point in your life?

List any behavior changes you could make to help you get your unmet needs met.

Name the topics or people that you stew about, are angry with, or are jealous of most often. What do people say or do that you react to most?

In these cases, what needs are not getting met?

What actions would be most beneficial for you to take at that time?

What prevents you from adopting these behaviors?

"There is no light without shadow and no psychic wholeness without imperfection."

—Carl Jung

Chapter 6

Returning to Wholeness: Owning Your Shadow

In Chapters 4 and 5 I talked about the behaviors we learn to protect us. It is useful to become aware of and understand some of our own motivations underneath our behaviors. Frequently our motivations are hidden even from ourselves, making it difficult to understand them. Is it really that important to understand our underlying motivations? If we are experiencing emotional pain or if we are seeking a deeper meaning in our lives, then the answer is yes.

One example of our hidden parts is the "human shadow." Carl Jung identified and then studied what he called the human shadow. The shadow includes the undeveloped potentials within us, as well as aspects of our personalities that we have buried and/or denied inside ourselves and often do not like.

The complexity and depth of the concepts of the unconscious, the soul, and the "human shadow" make it very difficult to describe in a short chapter in this book. My goal is to create a starting point and present a general "map" to begin exploration for those interested in creating more balance, meaning, and depth in their lives. Doing deep shadow work really is best accomplished in psychotherapy and in ceremonies. However I also see a benefit to reading and discussing Jung's concepts of the psyche.

In the book *Romancing the Shadow*, Connie Zweig and Steve Wolf write, "Beneath the social mask we wear every day, we have a hidden shadow side: an impulsive, wounded, sad, or isolated part that we generally try to ignore. The Shadow can be a source of emotional richness and vitality, and acknowledging it can be a pathway to healing and an authentic life. We meet our dark side, accept it for what it is, and we learn to use its powerful energies in productive ways. The shadow knows why good people sometimes do 'bad' things. Romancing the Shadow and learning to read the messages it encodes in daily life can deepen your consciousness, imagination, and soul."

These neglected parts are initially outside our awareness, residing in our unconscious, and can be both positive and negative in nature. Shadow parts involve opposite qualities in relation to our conscious minds and egos. As an example, if the ego wants to be strong, the shadow would include vulnerability or perceived weakness (as we shall see in this chapter). As Jung said, "The shadow is the negative side of the personality, the sum of all those unpleasant qualities we like to hide, together with the insufficiently developed functions and the contents of the personal unconscious."

The theory is that everyone has buried shadows. General examples of shadow include personality traits and potentials, feelings, attitudes, and beliefs. Specific examples are many: passivity, assertiveness, anger, fear, sexuality, patience, impatience, personal power, hatred, and love. Children will bury and deny their shadow parts for many reasons, but these parts don't vanish. Instead they remain hidden somewhere inside us.

Swiss Jungian psychologist and scholar Marie-Louise von Franz describes a practical reason for consciously choosing to acknowledge and integrate the shadow parts: "The expression 'assimilation of the shadow' is meant to apply to childish, primitive, undeveloped sides of one's nature." Integrating our shadow parts moves us toward living in our true nature of wholeness that I believe we were all born with. Connie Zweig further describes the benefits of integrating our personal shadow when she states, "As we begin to acknowledge hidden so-called negative traits—laziness, jealousy, impulsivity, self-centeredness—as well as undeveloped positive traits—creative talents, parenting skills, healing abilities—in our shadow figures, we expand the range of who we are. The shadow reveals its gold in creative works, which build bridges between the conscious and unconscious worlds. The arts have the power to loosen the tight grasp of the conscious mind, permitting unknown moods and images to arise. Writers and artists alike have helped to lift the veil and allow others a glimpse of the infinite riches of the shadow realm."

I believe the results of integrating the shadow help us gain the "wisdom of the wound." The reason we deny parts of ourselves is that, as children, we interpreted messages and perceived certain traits to be bad or wrong. As Jung explained it, "Children adjust to their adult surroundings." That is, children take cues to determine what qualities/traits are right and wrong, especially from their siblings and parents. Through their system of rewards and punishments, parents encourage and discourage certain traits and emotions in us. Many of the messages, both positive and negative, that parents give to their children are unintentional.

Let's take eight-year-old Brad as an example. Brad's parents want him to grow up to be strong at all costs. They want him to always be able to take care of himself as an adult, to stand up for and protect himself physically and emotionally. This is a positive wish for a child's development. Most parents want their children to grow up healthy and strong, and to be able to handle the challenges that life brings.

However, depending on how the parents approach these issues with Brad, they may also discourage his sensitivity, or squelch his vulnerability. Because many of the messages children receive are nonverbal and indirect, children are often left to interpret interactions and messages. Also, many parents' intentions and interactions are unconsciously transmitted to their children. Messages come in all shapes and forms, including mixed messages. How the child perceives them is further complicated by the make-up of the child and the family dynamics as a whole. When a child is left to guess, either in negative or ambiguous situations, he will often guess the worst about himself. This is especially true when families are chaotic or unsupportive, or when a child does not feel safe, confident, or supported.

Based on his interactions with his parents, Brad could easily conclude that being sensitive or passive is bad, even though these traits are in themselves neither good nor bad. In the family, Brad might be teased or ridiculed when he behaves passively or when he remains silent. Perhaps one of his parents was teased in childhood and protected himself or herself by withdrawing from siblings or classmates. Deep down the parent still carries the shame and guilt of feeling weak and helpless as a child, and wants life to be better for Brad.

As an example, when Brad's father sees Brad withdrawing from an interaction, he becomes silent and leaves the room. Alternatively, he may pressure Brad to be more assertive, either verbally (e.g., yelling) or nonverbally (e.g., with a meaningful glance). Either way Brad is faced with figuring out what to do to please his parents, or at least not to lose their positive attention. Not wanting to be judged as weak, Brad unconsciously buries his quiet and passive side along with his vulnerability, tolerance for silence, and listening skills. These repressed traits, now buried in his unconscious, become his shadow.

By not appearing weak, Brad is protecting himself, as well as pleasing his parents. While internally he struggles with interpreting and guessing at the interactions and messages from his family, Brad develops a "thick skin," which also helps him excel in academics and sports at school.

As Brad grows, so do his emotional wounds. Maybe the family attacks or ignores him whenever he is feeling sad or vulnerable, providing further "proof" to Brad that passivity and vulnerability are bad. He likely will hide his hurt feelings when teased by his family or friends, and continue to distance himself from his soft and vulnerable side to protect himself. Since his parents didn't validate or honor these traits in him, over time he abandons them in himself.

Outwardly, Brad moves forward in life, working hard at being a strong, competent person. But inwardly, sinking deeper into the unconscious, is the wounded child that others can't see. All the while, Brad's wounds are mounting up inside, along with a set of beliefs and fears. I call it the "wounded child's dictionary," full of inaccurate and all-or-nothing pictures and definitions about himself and the world. Some of Brad's general beliefs/definitions may include the following: *Passive people are weak. Being vulnerable is always wrong. Never be silent, quiet, or vulnerable.* He might manufacture personalized beliefs such as, *"I'm weak because sometimes I'm silent or vulnerable"* and *"Everyone will leave me because I'm weak."*

These beliefs grow out of the original wounding, becoming generalized to the rest of the world. The inner wounded child holds two universal and distinct energies: (1) all-or-nothing thinking and (2) hopelessness.

Possible *shadow parts* that Brad may bury include vulnerability, softness, listening, respect, and even fear. *Protective behaviors* may include aggressiveness, dominance in relationships, demeaning interactions, competence, and confidence (at least outwardly) in all actions.

Protecting the Wounds

Brad

Beliefs:
- Passivity is bad
- Vulnerability is wrong
- Always be agressive

Wounds
Loneliness,
Sadness, Grief

Protective Behaviors:
Agressive, Dominant,
Demeaning, Competent

Shadow Parts: Passivity, silent side, vulnerability

Diagram 14: Map to Awareness. Brads beliefs, wounds, protective behaviors, and shadow parts.

Beliefs formed in childhood often do protect the child in the environment in which they are formed. In Brad's example, he is encouraged and supported when he is bold and assertive. Always wanting to please his parents and to avoid ridicule, he learns his lessons well and practices boldness and assertion.

Yet as he grows into adulthood, these practices don't serve him the way they once did. The rest of the world doesn't respond to him exactly as his family did. But he is still behaving as he always has. He assumes that people expect him to be strong and he may fear that all people will see him and treat him as weak if he doesn't act strong, which is more all-or-nothing thinking. He doesn't consciously think these things in his adult, rational mind. Rather, these are fears that reside in the wounded child's memory, outside his awareness. We can predict that frustrations will grow out of this image he has of himself and the illusions he carries.

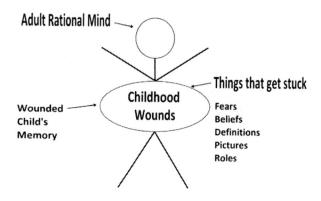

Diagram 15: Adult rational mind

Early Wounding

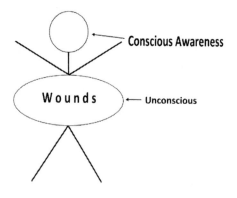

Diagram 16: Unconscious vs. Conscious Map

As Brad grows older, his needs may shift. His quiet and sensitive qualities may want an outlet. Therefore, a conflict arises in his adult relationships. He has a deep desire to be honest as well as vulnerable, and to be caring and trusting (the soul seeking wholeness), but he still has the old habits of protecting his vulnerability. Eventually the need for emotional closeness grows bigger than the need to protect his ego.

This is when things become uncomfortable. People ignore these needs for years and years, sometimes for a lifetime. But they will likely create a lot of pain for themselves because they will "get hit over the head" over and over again before they finally say "Enough! I can't do it this way any longer!"

Ignoring their needs for emotional closeness may come at the cost of losing or harming important relationships. As difficult as it is to confront the beliefs, attitudes, and energies buried in the shadow, the potential rewards are huge. I believe Jung captures it well when he says, "Owning up to the shadow is not nearly as damaging in the long run as denying it."

So Brad has choices. He can decide to penetrate the surface of his strong image and tough exterior with the light of awareness, and experience his own vulnerability. This isn't easy. In fact, it will be painful. Besides grieving, I don't believe there is anything more painful than to turn and face our shadows. Challenging the old definitions from our past and getting in touch with our buried gifts requires a form of death and rebirth. Accepting this kind of inner death, I believe, supports a certain kind of surrender, which can lead to freedom.

The challenge is available to all of us. The reward is wholeness, or at least moving toward wholeness. We can discover buried parts of ourselves and learn to accept these parts and live in harmony with them. This is the wisdom of the wound. In other words, we can live with more balance and health, wholeness, and richness. Ultimately these undeveloped parts of us want to shine.

Brad is faced with a conflict: vulnerability vs. assertiveness/aggression. Perhaps they are the needs of the soul (to become whole) vs. the needs of the ego (to always present a strong front). As he grows older, Brad's needs for closeness and support grow as large as the need to be seen as strong. At that point his needs create a painful conflict inside him. If he does not change, he will encounter "fate."

Jung stated, "That which we do not deal with consciously will show up in our lives as fate." It may appear in the form of an addiction, loss of a job, breakup of a relationship, or something else that will pull him into his grief and his vulnerability. Brad will then be forced to face this conflict and pain. Yet the reward of facing his shadow is wholeness and living his own truth, not someone else's truth from long ago.

If he decides to consciously look at his shadow he can expect discomfort, to put it mildly. When we first come into contact with these parts of ourselves, we feel pain. I call it "awareness and the cringe," and it happens every time someone turns and faces his shadow. When Brad lifts up his passive, quiet, and vulnerable traits and holds them in front of his face, he will cringe. No question. At one time he labeled them "bad" or "wrong." That label is still there in his unconscious.

The traits that Brad "majored in"—i.e., assertiveness, aggression, and strength—served him well. Many people fear losing these traits when they learn to accept their shadow parts. They say, "I don't want to give up those parts of myself," or "If I'm not the person I thought I was, then who am I?" But Brad does not need to give up these traits. He will never lose them and will never forget how to live using these qualities. They are natural gifts from his personality and spirit, but now they don't have to define him.

He can learn to live in both worlds, in his wholeness. Jung states, "The shadow also displays a number of good qualities such as normal instincts, appropriate reactions, realistic insights, creative impulses, etc." This is the wisdom of the wound. It may seem as if he needs to *change* who he is. In reality, he just needs to *accept* who he is, accept more parts of himself.

The buried parts within us get restless and resentful over time and eventually try to find their way out. The passive side looks to come out of an assertive person. Anger tries to find a way out of an easygoing person. Grief looks for an opening. The child wants to play inside of a serious adult. A "savior" caregiver wants to be supported. An angry grouch needs to be sad. The "life of the party" feels lonely and disconnected. Which ones am I missing? Any others come to mind?

Here is one final example of buried wounds and shadow. Barb grew up in a large family in which she was neglected by emotionally wounded and passive parents. All negative emotions and conflicts were repressed and avoided in her family. As a child, Barb interpreted this to mean that anger and conflict were bad and to be avoided, and she learned to deny her own anger and negative emotions.

She learned to take care of her parents, and to feel responsible for their unhappiness. Because her own needs were neglected and she felt responsible for her parents' happiness, she developed negative beliefs about herself and narrow definitions about relationships.

Barb grew into adulthood never seeing her own emotional needs as a priority. She also found many friends (and family) to take care of. She married a man with rage problems and a disinclination to work. She constantly rescued him and covered for him. Many of her behaviors were supportive and positive and in her mind she was doing them because "he had a bad childhood."

Protecting the Wounds

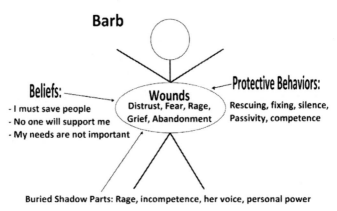

Beliefs:
- I must save people
- No one will support me
- My needs are not important

Wounds
Distrust, Fear, Rage,
Grief, Abandonment

Protective Behaviors:
Rescuing, fixing, silence,
Passivity, competence

Buried Shadow Parts: Rage, incompetence, her voice, personal power

Diagram 17: Map of Awareness: Barbara's wounding

Unconsciously she is still trying to rescue one or both of her parents, which is her definition of being a "good person." Part of her *shadow* may include rage, grief, and personal power. By attempting to save people, she is really trying to save herself. However, she unconsciously still holds the outdated and inaccurate belief that if she puts her needs first, she is being selfish. However, if she chooses to shine light on her shad-

ow parts, and learns to accept them, she will learn to love herself. She can keep all of her supportive behaviors, and support
her own needs as well.

"Fear" is a liar. It takes our choice away without our even
knowing. I like to say, "Fear comes and steals our choice, and
Awareness takes it back." To become aware we must not deny
our fear, but rather face it and learn from it. We are either allowing or resisting. We are either swimming upstream or flowing downstream at any given moment. If we allow all of our
thoughts, emotions, and fears to surface, we can respond to
them in a healthier way. If we try to push them deeper inside of
us to protect us, we create a pushback, and develop greater
problems. But we can take back the power of choice when we
live with awareness and intention.

The Buddhists say, "Live your life as an experiment." Here
is a question you can ask yourself: "What can I let go of today?" Ask this question every day. Other questions to ask:
"Am I allowing or resisting right now?" "What am I protecting
or resisting that I don't need anymore, such as anger, fear,
stubbornness, resentment, selfishness, silence, sadness, safe-
ty?" And then rephrase the answer into a statement of intention, such as "Just for today, I choose to let go of my
_____." (Fill in the blank.) The important word is
"choose."

There will always be blind spots in our vision, in our
awareness. That's the challenge. With the practice of awareness we can improve our skills at seeing what our internal obstacles are, including our fears and shadow parts. We know that
awareness is crucial to a full life but how do you practice it?
Practice sitting silently observing your thoughts, feelings, fears,

and desires. Practice observing your inner world while you are interacting with others. With time you will move past discomfort and into self-acceptance, discovering your deepest needs and desires beyond the ego. It's a practice of witnessing, validating, and loving yourself and honoring all parts of yourself. This kind of allowing supports you returning to your wholeness and thriving.

"Ring the bells that can ring. Forget your perfect offering.
There's a crack in everything, that's how the light gets in."
—Leonard Cohen

Chapter 6: Review

As Jung says, "The shadow is the negative side of the personality, the sum of all those unpleasant qualities we like to hide, together with the insufficiently developed functions and the contents of the personal unconscious."

Reasons we bury parts of ourselves:

- We've been trained. As kids, we received or perceived messages that these parts are bad or wrong.

- We associate them with past negative experiences, such as punishment or withdrawal of love or affection.

- We believe that these parts of ourselves will be hurtful, or that people will leave us because of them.

- To protect our wounds and ourselves.

Why we retrieve the shadow parts of ourselves:

- To honor them.

- To become whole again.

- To learn to accept all parts of ourselves—to love our-selves.

"Fear is a natural reaction to moving closer to the truth."
—Pema Chodron

Chapter 6: Worksheet

Protecting the Wounds

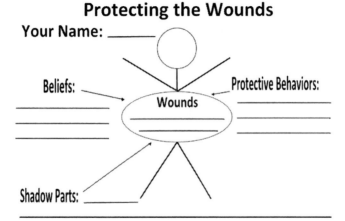

Map of your awareness:

Use the diagram above to help you answer the Chapter 6 worksheet questions to explore your buried shadow parts.

Buried shadow parts can include many varied things, such as passivity, assertiveness, anger, fear, a sex drive, patience, impatience, personal power, hatred, love, hope, our voice, the masculine, the feminine, and more.

What are some possible shadow parts that you have buried?

Were there judgments or messages from childhood about these traits or parts? If so, what were they?

What personality traits have you "majored in"? (What are your dominant and most common ways you "act out"?)

Have you ever been surprised at how you responded to a given situation (in thoughts, words, or actions)? If so, what were the thoughts, words, or actions? (They may be messages from your undeveloped sides.)

Name an activity that you have avoided.

Are there any old messages, judgments, or family sayings connected to this activity? If so, what are they?

Are these judgments accurate? Would you like to change the messages or judgments? How can you do this?

In what ways were you disrespected in childhood?

List the behaviors you used to respond to the disrespect? Do you still use them? Do they still serve you?

Describe some behaviors with which you could replace them.

"In the night of death, hope sees a star, and listening love can hear the rustle of a wing."

—Robert Ingersoll

Chapter 7

The Art of Allowing

When we avoid our emotional wounding (including our buried shadow parts), and when we don't take the conscious and intentional healing path inward, we end up unconsciously allowing the ego to be in charge of protecting and responding to the wounds. This will create negative and sometimes devastating results.

We can look at the goals and symptoms of the ego to understand its limiting effects in protecting our wounds. The ego wants to avoid any pain (real or imagined) at all costs and wants others to see us in a good light. It also will take the shortest path to this end, creating negative consequences. It may relieve pain in the moment but cause more problems in the future.

When the ego tries to avoid pain, we will stuff our greatest pain (such as grief, fear, and anguish) deeper inside and move forward. The unresolved inner conflict results in neurosis, which Jung described as "a significant unresolved tension between opposing attitudes of the ego and the unconscious." Symptoms of neurosis include anxiety, depression, fear, resentment, compulsivity, and even righteousness. Jung identified this dynamic when he stated, "Neurosis is always a substitute for legitimate suffering." I interpret "legitimate suffering" to mean grieving, as well as allowing and accepting every feeling and response to our experiences. Jung also defined neurosis as "suffering that has not found its meaning."

I listed one of the symptoms of neurosis as righteousness. At some time in our childhood we may appoint ourselves one or two specific "jobs" that represent who we are, and protect our wounded selves. These jobs, or roles, are formed out of our personalities, family dynamics, and experiences, and the ego is in charge. The jobs represent who we are in our persona (self-image) and are connected to our value and importance, in a limited definition of ourselves through the ego's eyes.

Because the jobs help define us and protect the ego and wounds, unconsciously we believe we must become the "very best" at these jobs. This is where our belief in righteousness develops. Because of the all-or-nothing thinking of our wounded selves we become afraid that if we are not the best at our roles we will be unlovable and not valued.

Examples of the roles/jobs that we choose include: best caregiver, hardest worker, most generous, smartest, best problem solver, fairest, best behaved, bravest, least needy, most loving, funniest, strongest, most forgiving, etc. They are positive and useful roles and actions. But if we are dependent upon them for our value or importance, we will eventually compulsively cling to them out of fear. It's important to remember that we never lose these traits and abilities. Through emotional healing we learn to love *all* parts of ourselves. Then we treasure our unique gifts without the need or compulsion to defend or prove ourselves.

The healing path will lead us through the wounds, where we witness our full selves, including the shadow. Through this process we learn to accept the other parts of ourselves. "Legitimate suffering" is also found on the healing path. The path always includes an inward and downward trip, and I believe it is the scariest path we can take. Jung said, "People will do anything, no matter how absurd, in order to avoid facing their own soul." Taking the path inward requires passing through doors of vulnerability with fear as the starting point.

As Jung said, "The road to consciousness is through the wound." By taking the sacred journey through the wounds, we shine the light of awareness into the unconscious. We discover and eventually accept and love more parts of ourselves that we, as children, egocentrically labeled bad or wrong. There are many ways we can take this path. Some of them include psychotherapy, life coaching, through ritual and ceremony, with teachers, mentors, and spiritual guides. We can utilize experiential work, using "active imagination," music, and all the arts.

Abraham-Hicks (Law of Allowing) states, "Worthiness, in very simple terms, means I have found a way to let the Energy reach me, the Energy that is natural, to reach me. Worthiness, or unworthiness, is something that is pronounced upon you by you. You are the only one who can love yourself into a state of allowing, or hate yourself into a state of disallowing."

Wholeness is our natural state at birth. When we let go and **allow** ourselves to take the path inward and flow with the river, instead of struggling against the current out of fear, we will release our wounded energy and change our negative beliefs and definitions about the world and ourselves. We will reclaim our buried shadow parts, thus returning to our wholeness.

This is how we gain the "Wisdom of the Wound."

"The soul moves through life with grace. The ego moves through life with recklessness, chaos, and drama. The ego tirelessly swims against the current, while the soul sits back and floats in the direction that life is moving in. You're either being guided by your soul or driven by your ego. At any time, you have access to either of these realities."

—Debbie Ford

"Authentic power is when the personality aligns with the Soul."

—Gary Zukav

Summary Goals

Identification of your blocks to thriving and moving downstream. These blocks may include negative thoughts, negative beliefs, pictures, definitions, and any behaviors that limit our creation and thriving in life. They may also include past traumatic experiences.

- Healing of grief, wounding, emotions, and traumas.

- Creating the life you want through a broad picture of your life, as well as being conscious in your daily and moment-to-moment lives.

- Creating and maintaining some type of practice of ritual, ceremony, and mindfulness practice, especially the practice of positive and creative thoughts, beliefs, definitions, and daily habits of thriving. This can include allowing any and all thoughts, feelings, and energy to flow freely rather than resisting them, which creates a false need to protect or defend them.

- Choosing supportive people for your life who witness your authentic self, people who support your uniqueness and creation.

- Choosing people who will guide you and support you; mentors, teachers, a life coach, and/or a psychotherapist, a spiritual guide.

Theories used in this book and my work:

- Jungian psychology

- Cognitive Behavioral Therapy

- Law of Attraction-Allowing

- Attachment theory

- Mindfulness

- Taoism

- Buddhism

Suggested authors/writers: Specific books are listed in the Suggested Resources.

Abraham-Hicks

Thich Naht Hahn

Carl Jung

Marion Woodman

Robert Bly

Don Miguel Ruiz

James Hollis

Linda Leonard

The Dalai Lama

Reed Wilson

Albert Ellis

Pema Chodron

Rumi

Anam Thubten

James Hillman

Lao Tzu

Glossary of Jungian Terms
Taken from http://carl-jung.net/glossary.html

Active imagination: Method of assimilation of unconscious contents through their experimentation as fantasies in the wakeful state.

Anima: The archetype of female in man.

Animus: The archetype of male in woman.

Archetype: Primary structural element of human psyche. The archetype equals biologists' pattern of behavior as it rules the functioning of the psychical process.

Archetypal Image: The form or representation taken by the archetype in dreams, fantasies, cultural and religious (mythical) products.

Compensation: A natural process of reestablishing a certain balance in the psyche.

Consciousness: The waking condition; knowing what is happening around oneself; the state of being conscious.

Ego: The central complex in the field of consciousness. (See also Self.)

Individuation: Complex process of synthesis of the Self, which consists mainly of the unconscious with the conscious.

Inflation: Following the identification with an archetypal image, the effect of this identification is to exaggerate the proportions of the Ego.

Neurosis: A significant unresolved tension between opposing attitudes of the ego and the unconscious.

Persona: Mask of the Ego, it is social expression, the way the others see us.

Personal unconscious: The Freudian unconscious, made of repressed wishes, distinctive from the collective (archetypal) unconscious.

Projection: Autonomous process by which features (usually repressed) of the ego are assigned to other people (external objects).

Psyche: The totality of all psychological processes, both conscious and unconscious.

Shadow: Hidden or unconscious aspects of ourselves. Both good and bad, which the ego has either repressed or never recognized. Containing repressed parts of the human personality, the shadow is the counterpart of the Freudian unconscious. The shadow is the archetypal content.

Self: The archetype of psychic Totality, according to Jung.

Wholeness: Psychic stage in which the union of the unconscious with the conscious has been achieved. It is the aim of Jung's psychotherapy.

Suggested Resources

I *would encourage the reader to search for other books by the* *authors that are recommended, in addition to the specific* *books I have referenced here.*

Bly, Robert (1998). *A Little Book on the Human Shadow*. San Francisco: Harper San Francisco (http://robertbly.com)

Carter, Forrest (1976, 2004). *The Education of Little Tree*. New York: The Delacorte Press

Chodron, Pema (1997). *When Things Fall Apart*. Boston: Shambhala Publications Inc.
(http://pemachodronfoundation.org)

Hicks, Esther and Jerry (2004). *Ask and it is Given*. Carlsbad, CA: Hay House Inc. (www.abraham-hicks.com)

Hillman, James (1996). *The Soul's Code: In Search of Character and Calling*. New York: Warner Books Inc. (http://www.mythosandlogos.com/Hillman.html)

Hollis, James (2001). *Creating a Life: Finding Your Individual Path*. Toronto: Inner City Books.
(http://www.jameshollis.net/books/default.htm)

Johnson, Robert (1996). *Inner Work: Using Dreams and Active Imagination for Personal Growth*. San Francisco: Harper San Francisco (http://www.wholenesstherapy.com)

Jung, Carl Gustav (1961, 1962, 1963). *Memories, Dreams, Reflections.* New York: Random House Inc. (http://cgjungpage.org) (http://carl-jung.net)

Lao Tzu (1998). *Tao Tae Ching.* Mitchel, Stephen New York: Harper Collins (http://www.chebucto.ns.ca/Philosophy/Taichi/lao.html)

Leonard, Linda (1989). *Witness to the Fire: Creativity and the Veil of Addiction.* Boston, Massachusetts, Shambhala Publications Inc. (http://thebrainpan.wordpress.com/2009/05/13/linda-leonard-author-and-jungian-analyst)

Moore, Robert. Gillette, Douglas (1990). *King, Warrior, Magician, Lover: Rediscovering the Archetypes of the Mature Masculine.* New York: Harper Collins Publisher (http://robertmoore-phd.com)

Ruiz, Don Miguel (1997) *The Four Agreements: A Practical Guide to Personal Freedom (A Toltec Wisdom Book).* San Rafael, California: Amber-Allen Publishing Inc. (http://newagreementsforlife.com/register.html)

Stein, Murray (1998, 1999, 2001, 2003). *Jung's Map of the Soul: An Introduction.* Chicago: Open Court Publishing Company (http://www.murraystein.com/midway.html)

Thich Naht Hahn (2001). *You are Here.* Boston: Shambhala Publications Inc. (http://www.plumvillage.org/thich-nhat-hanh.html)

Thubten, Anam (2012*). The Magic of Awareness.* Snow Lion Publications (http://www.dharmata.org)

Von Franz, Marie-Louise. Kennedy, William H. (1980). *Projection and Re-Collection in Jungian Psychology: Reflections of the Soul.* Peru, Ill: Open Court Publishing Company. (http://marie-louisevonfranz.com/en/books.html)

Wilson, Reid (1987). *Don't Panic: Taking Control of Anxiety Attacks.* New York: Harper Collins (http://www.anxieties.com/about.php#.UUFlWO3iM20)

Woodman, Marion (1982). *Addiction to Perfection: The Still Unravished Bride: A Psychological Study.* Toronto, Canada: Inner City Books (http://www.mwoodmanfoundation.org)

Zweig, Connie; Wolf, Steve (1991). *Romancing the Shadow: A Guide to Soul Work for a Vital, Authentic Life.* New York: The Random House Publishing Group (http://conniezweig.com)

Zukav, Gary (1989). *The Seat of the Soul.* New York: Fireside Publications by Simon and Schuster (http://seatofthesoul.com)

Workshops

I conduct workshops and give presentations on the material in this book for all those who wish to heal their emotional wounds from the past, and then change their behaviors to become whole, healthy, adults.

I present two-hour lectures, half-day workshops, and full day workshops.

Although I prefer to conduct my workshops in my home city, Bozeman, MT., in the beautiful Rocky Mountains, 90 miles north of Yellowstone Park, arrangements can be negotiated for workshops in other locations upon group request.

Topics covered:

- Identifying the blocks to emotional wholeness

- Identifying unconscious beliefs underneath destructive behaviors

- Family roles and development of our persona

I also present workshops for agencies and other businesses on the following topics:

- Personality conflicts within the systems/offices

- Conflict resolution

- Healing retreats, with experiential healing of emotional wounding

- Improving communication with partners and coworkers.

For more information go to my website:
www.neilbricco.com

Or contact me at:

Email: neilbricco@hotmail.com

Telephone: (406) 581-9097

Acknowledgements

There were many people who influenced the writing and the creation of this book.

To Anna Goodwin, my colleague and friend. Your tireless and great work and your nudging support allowed me to finish this book. It simply would not have gotten published without you. I am grateful for you.

To Ron Goodwin, Anna's husband, who volunteered to read and provide feedback and support. Many thanks Ron.

To the board and the entire staff of Bitterroot Mountain Publishing LLC. Thank you for providing a vehicle for first time writers like myself to launch books.

To Steve Kirchhoff, Phil Heron, Sarah Ridge, Jenny Leo, my friends and colleagues who edited my book at different stages. You are all appreciated.

To all my clients throughout the years who made the painful and difficult choice to seek help. The healing path is not an easy road. Your courage to grieve and heal has influenced many of the ideas and concepts that I've highlighted in this book. Thank you.

To Nick Hammen and Deb Schmit, my dear friends. We've been through all kinds of weather, and I thank you for every moment. You inspire me through living an authentic life.

To Denise Dahl, my longtime friend, you listened to many of my "writes and re-writes" and encouraged me all the way. But mostly I thank you for your fairness and mutual love of creation.

To Nancy Stetter, my downstream friend. For the many mutual stories of thriving, I am grateful.

To Kathy Kinman, my good friend. Your practice of witnessing is the greatest gift you give to others.

To Rebecca Kinman. The sharing of visions is good medicine. And sometimes the Sun changes his mind. Thanks.

To Ron Voelker, my longtime friend, thanks for your support, hard work, brainstorming, and encouragement. And mostly thanks for being my friend.

To Rita Messmore, my new friend and colleague. Thank you for showing me another form of witnessing and healing.

To Julie Probus-Schad, for the Esalen experience, and for breathing fresh air and hope into this work.

To Pam Roberts, for your documentary films, and for helping create a vision for workshops.

To my "picking" friends John Drake, Bill Bradshaw, and Dan Lindly, for all the great music. You were a great diversion and source of rejuvenation!

To Neal Madson, Sheridan County Drug Court, for giving me the opportunity to start up an outpatient treatment program, and for giving me the freedom to create.

To Jerry Vanderpan, Kevin McNelis, and Jude Rowe who gave me my first job in Montana. Much appreciated!

To Kathy Dobberpuhl, my longtime friend. Thanks for the years of processing life, death, and health.

To Becky Burns and her children Stacie, Sarah, and Tom. Thank you for your generosity during a transition time.

To Dave Ditter, for your early counseling and guidance, and for supporting my dreams.

To Ken Morrison, who first challenged my old and neurotic ways and supported my best self. Thank you for showing me how to live in wholeness.

To Thomas Yellowtail, Sundance Chief of the Crow Nation, for taking me in and introducing me to the sacred ceremonies of your Native people. You walked me back to my spiritual path.

To Steve Yapuncich, my adopted brother. Through your unwavering commitment to spirit and the serving path, you helped me find my own spiritual path. Aho

To Thomas Ray "TR" Glenn, my Crow brother, who gave me a new name. You carried a heavy responsibility and blazed your own trail.

To Larson Medicine Horse, Ben Cloud, David Yarlott, Curtis One Bear, Kenny Wyles, Thomas "Hawk" Yellowtail, and Brad Crooked Arm, my Sundance and spiritual brothers. Aho

To Albert Bellante and Gena Bellante-Funk, my early psychotherapists who taught me Jungian psychology through my own healing.

To my friends who wandered with me into adulthood: Robbi Dreifuerst, Kathy Dobberpuhl, Randy Nielsen, Cheri Bricco, Paul Reiser, Andy Bricco, Robin Bricco, Wally Melchior, Cheryl Stern and Lynn Carlson. We had a lot of fun.

To Eddie Biebel, my long ago friend. You were the first person in my young life I witnessed following his own bliss. Thank you for all the music and inspiration you created.

To Gus Knollenberg and John Baitinger, my graduate school friends. Thanks for all the times we studied together, the insights, and the laughs we shared.

To Bob Van Gompel, an early teacher and coach. You were one of the first people in my childhood who saw something in me, told others about me, and then told me about me; a huge lesson in validation. This lesson still impacts my life.

CPSIA information can be obtained at www.ICGtesting.com
Printed in the USA
LVOW13s0038300913

354556LV00006B/95/P